MY FAVOURITE SHIRT

A HISTORY OF BEN SHERMAN STYLE

PAOLO HEWITT & TERRY RAWLINGS

PUBLISHED BY: BEN SHERMAN GROUP LIMITED 2 EYRE STREET HILL,CLERKENWELL,LONDON EC1R 5ET, UK © 2004 BEN SHERMAN GROUP LIMITED.

ISBN: 0-9548106-1-9 (hardback) ISBN: 0-9548106-0-0 (paperback) PRODUCT CODE: BS10001

DESIGNED BY: PAUL McEVOY @ BOLD GRAPHIC DESIGN, LONDON WITH TERRY RAWLINGS

CO-ORDINATED & COMPILED BY: TERRY RAWLINGS

RESEARCH BY: ANGELA CHARLES, DAPHNE SHERMAN, SARAH FEENEY, ANDY RIGG

EXCLUSIVE UK. DISTRIBUTORS: BOOK SALES LTD, 8/9 FRITH STREET, LONDON W1V 5TZ, UK.

TO THE MUSIC TRADE ONLY: MUSIC SALES LTD, 8/9 FRITH STREET, LONDON W1V 5TZ, UK.

PRINTED IN SPAIN
A CATALOGUE RECORD FOR THIS BOOK IS AVAILABLE FROM THE BRITISH LIBRARY.

THIS BOOK IS DEDICATED TO THE MEMORY OF BEN SHERMAN 1925 - 1987

"The high point years were probably four or five years before they became famous because that's when the factories were producing revolutionary merchandise.
There had simply never ever been anything like it on the English scene before, never! Revolutionary!"

BILL KNIGHTSBRIDGE
EMPLOYEE OF BEN SHERMAN
1963 - 1969

Ben Sherman®

SONS OF FRED c1965

Ben Sherman

"The atmosphere was euphoric, this really was 'Great Britain' and we were now the world leaders in everything from fashion to music."
DAPHNE SHERMAN

"I first came across Ben Sherman when I was at school in the early 70s. I really liked the fine details, like the buttons and the bright colours the shirts came in, especially the checks - to me the Ben Sherman label is bold and speaks up for itself without being in your face. It lives forever - no matter what era, there's a place for Ben Sherman."
LINFORD CHRISTIE: ATHLETE

FOREWORD

With hands clenched into a white knuckled fist 'the man' jumped out of his car. Mad with rage, uncontrollable anger had twisted his face into a frightening grotesque expression. Moving swiftly to the rear of his vehicle he was eager to face the person whom he considered had totally ruined his day. However, the other driver was more than ready for him. A head on clash between the two men seemed to be inevitable.

Suddenly, the offending driver said to his more than burly opponent, "That's a nice shirt!" Immediately upon hearing a compliment in his taste and style of dress, the angered man relaxed. Unclenching his fists, his terse lips spread into a wide smile, his friendly reply was, "It's a Ben Sherman."

So the very first of a series of Ben Sherman television commercials was broadcast across the United Kingdom.

Ben Sherman was built on the solid foundations of ingenuity, determination and persistency, together with the energy put into many hours of work. These were the deciding factors responsible for the popularity of the Ben Sherman Original shirt.

People often commented on Ben's success, but my husband would always reply with "I got lucky". This modest reply always left the enquirer wondering what exactly was the special ingredient responsible for his success? The one that Ben was keeping only to himself?

Was it the easy to iron Oxford cotton? The choice of so many colours? Or was it the soft roll of the button-down collar with the distinctive loop and pleat at the back? Maybe it was the specialised stitching, the comfort, or how it made one feel to be wearing a Ben Sherman Original.

Timing is everything, and my husband's timing could not have been more perfect. In 1963 the first Ben Sherman shirts entered the fashion scene, and quickly became an integral part of the 'swinging sixties'. Apart from the 'soul sounds' coming from the USA, the rest of the best came from the UK. The Beatles sang it, and we did it.

We were all on our own 'Magical Mystery Tour' and some of us actually did turn off, relax and float downstream. We swooned when we heard Tom Jones sing 'It's Not Unusual' and we celebrated for weeks after England's football captain Bobby Moore lifted the World Cup. We were passionate about our football, and George Best became everyone's darling and a fifth Beatle to boot.

The atmosphere was euphoric, this really was 'Great Britain' and we were now the world leaders in everything from fashion to music.

In celebration of my late husband and the legacy he has left to the world of fashion that has lasted for more than four decades, I feel honoured and delighted to have taken part in putting this book together.

A special thank you goes to everyone in this book who gave their own individual stories and photographs to say and show how they feel about Ben Sherman.

DAPHNE SHERMAN.

INTRODUCTION

It's about time we woke up to the fact that we now live in a day and age where just about anyone can launch a personalised range of 'something or other' on an unsuspecting public, seemingly overnight. It could be a soap star's monogrammed line in lingerie, a TV chef's assortment of casserole dishes or a footballer's wife's favourite fragrance. It's a consumer's market, and it's all out there, jostling for shelf space, and hoping to entice us.

If these initialled desirables are one of a few things - aesthetically pleasing, top quality, or even good old fashioned 'value for money' - then they may just go the distance with an increasingly fickle public. Most, however, won't and indeed don't... 90% are usually as transient and have as fleeting a marketable presence as some of their creators' respective careers. It's not surprising, therefore, that truly classic designs are becoming a fondly remembered thing of the past.

Aaah - but it wasn't always that way. Once upon a time this proud little island of ours prided itself in aspiring to manufacture style icons by the shedload - think: Concorde, Rolls Royce, Mini Cooper, Hovercraft, HP Sauce and Colman's Mustard (the powdered variety, naturally). Now Concorde and Hovercraft are gone, the Germans own Rolls Royce and the Mini, and the French have robbed us of HP Sauce! OK, we still have the mustard, but for how long?

Thankfully our fashion industry has fared much better, and is still as interesting and varied as it was back in its widely recognised heyday of the 1960s. Yes... that magical era when England 'swung like a pendulum do', and London in particular finally cast aside the cold grey apparel of its ration book years... and like that scene from the Wizard of Oz suddenly turned technicolor! Teenagers were buying white Levi's, and dyeing them bright yellow and pink. Suede boots came in various hues of blue and green and the button down shirt became THE most desirable, essential and versatile purchase of all.

High fashion emporiums like John Stephen, Lord John and Granny Takes A Trip may have long since closed up shop but Carnaby Street and the Kings Road still attract the sartorially elegant, bright young things as much today as they always did. Of course, brand names still command the hard currency of the high street and have continued to garner commercial success through the decades. Some have even become interwoven into the fabric of British culture, and none more so than the one and only Ben Sherman. It's a name that stands out like a beacon and as a testament to enduring, evolving quality and tastefulness it is as culturally important as anything this country has ever produced. Like all great classics, Ben Sherman is timeless. Or to borrow a quote from another old favourite British brand - *"It's as good today as it's always been."*

This book will hopefully go some way into highlighting the significance and sheer pride of place Ben Sherman still holds in great British hearts, let alone their wardrobes.

TERRY RAWLINGS

"I got my absolute
favourite Ben Sherman second
hand from the Portobello Road in 1977.
It was a blue-green check and it was
fucking gorgeous with white Levis -
I loved that shirt. Getting that look right got me
my first job at Decca Records and I wore it to
death, until it literally fell apart. All too often
I'd be ironing that shirt dry in front of the telly
on a Saturday evening, just so I could wear it
to that night's gig - The Jam or The Nips
or a band of that ilk - or so I could look
the nuts on that night's date.
Fabulous times - fabulous shirts."

GARY CROWLEY:
DJ & PRESENTER

"My shirts are a part of youth culture, crossing over generations."

BEN SHERMAN

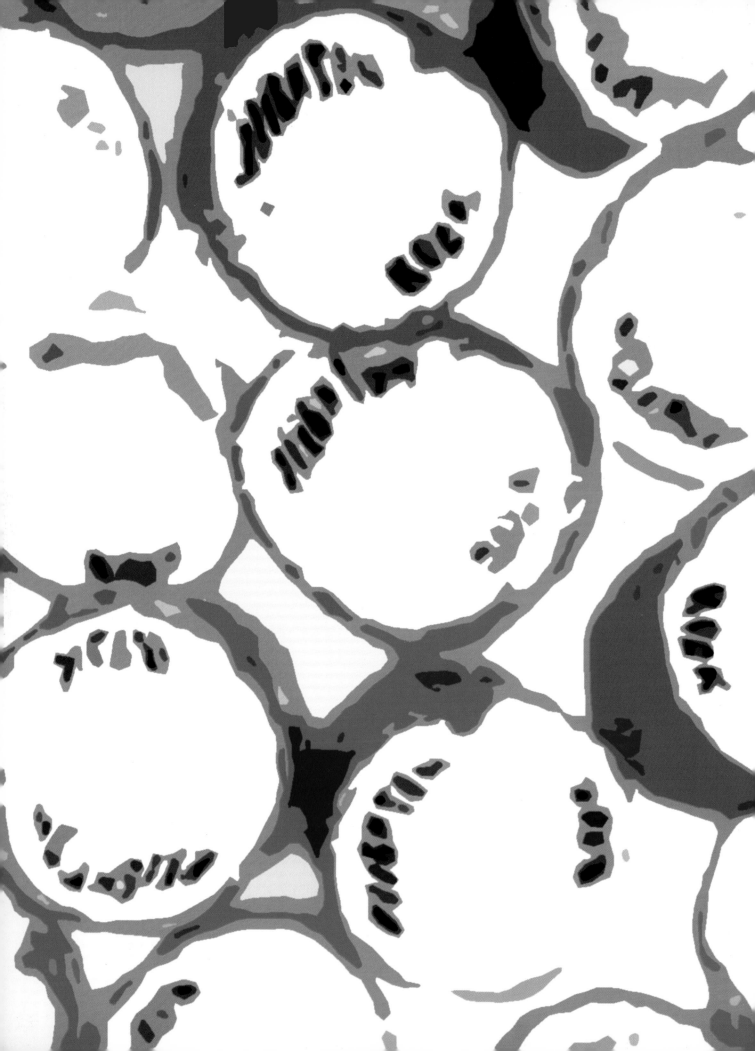

SUCK IT AND SEE

Just months after the Second World War ended, a twenty-year old man named Arthur Benjamin Sugarman packed up his belongings and boarded a ship for Canada, final destination, America. It was 1946. Europe was in complete economic and financial disarray, shattered by the Second World War. America on the other hand was a buoyant economic force. Unemployment was low, the standard of living rising dramatically.

No wonder Arthur was irresistibly drawn to this huge expanse of land and dreams. England was too small, too parochial for Arthur. He knew he had the makings of a great salesman and he knew America was the only place to make him his fortune.

Emigration always requires tough courage, especially in 1946 when travel was the preserve of the rich and leaving your country was a subject few even thought about.

This audacious mission tells us much about Arthur's character.

He began his journey from his hometown of Brighton, the town he was born in on October 3rd, 1925. His family had a history of heart problems and Arthur was no exception. He was born with slight heart trouble but then he never let any physical concern, including his hard-to-control weight, stand in the way of his drive or ambition.

His parents owned a shop called Rocko's Fancy Goods which was situated close to Brighton train station (it was on the right hand side as you exited). Originally, the family sold rock and sweets (their slogan was 'Suck It And See') before entering the pawnbroker business. When many of their customers failed to claim back their goods, the Sugarman family turned the premises into a bric-a-brac shop.

FROM TOP:
ROCKO'S BEACH HUT, ROCKO'S FANCY GOODS SHOP, BOY BEN, BEN'S BARMITZVAH, BEN ADOPTING THE DASHING DAVID NIVEN LOOK

"We had to find shirts
that went with those bleeding
red hunting jackets the Kinks wore.
I remember all the shirts being polka
dots at one point, which didn't go at all.
And then there were the ones with the
high collars which I couldn't wear either -
'cos I just haven't got a long neck, so we
ended up wearing those shirts with the
ruffle down the front, which looked like
blouses! When we discovered Ben
Shermans they were a great find -
they went with everything.
Nice shirts indeed."
MICK AVORY:
THE KINKS

THE KINKS. CLOCKWISE FROM LEFT: MICK AVORY, PETER QUAIFE, RAY DAVIES, DAVE DAVIES

Naturally, Arthur's father wanted his son to take over the business but after finishing his education and surviving the Second World War, Arthur declined the offer and made his move. He headed out to America.

As he made his way across the continent of his dreams, he took on a series of jobs. In Atlantic City, he worked as a salesman on its famous boardwalk and by night he was a waiter who serenaded the evening customers with a variety of songs. At one point he even became a tobacco picker and claimed it was the hardest job he ever took on.

He married twice but by the time he got to Los Angeles (he loved heat, hated the cold, so headed for the California sun) in 1953, he was single again. Which is why, on a Los Angeles beach, he was able to meet and fall in love with his third wife, Ruth Sherman. They quickly married and a son Daniel was born the next year. Another son Martin (named in honour of Arthur's favourite film, Marty) followed on December 30th, 1955. The family lived in the San Fernando Valley. Arthur worked for Ruth's father Aaron Minken, a very successful clothes manufacturer whose clothing empire had already created two hugely popular swimwear outlets, 'California Swimwear' and 'City Girl', both vibrant companies to this day.

Aaron took it upon himself to single-handedly teach his son-in-law every aspect of the business. He showed him how to manufacture clothes, how to market them, how to sell them. He taught him how business works, what to look for, where the traps are, how to win. Without Aaron Minken to guide him, it is fair to say that Arthur Sugarman's life would have been markedly different.

"My father learned so much from him," his son, Martin states. "If not for my grandfather, the whole line would never have been started."

"If not for my grandfather, the whole line would never have been started."

MARTIN SHERMAN

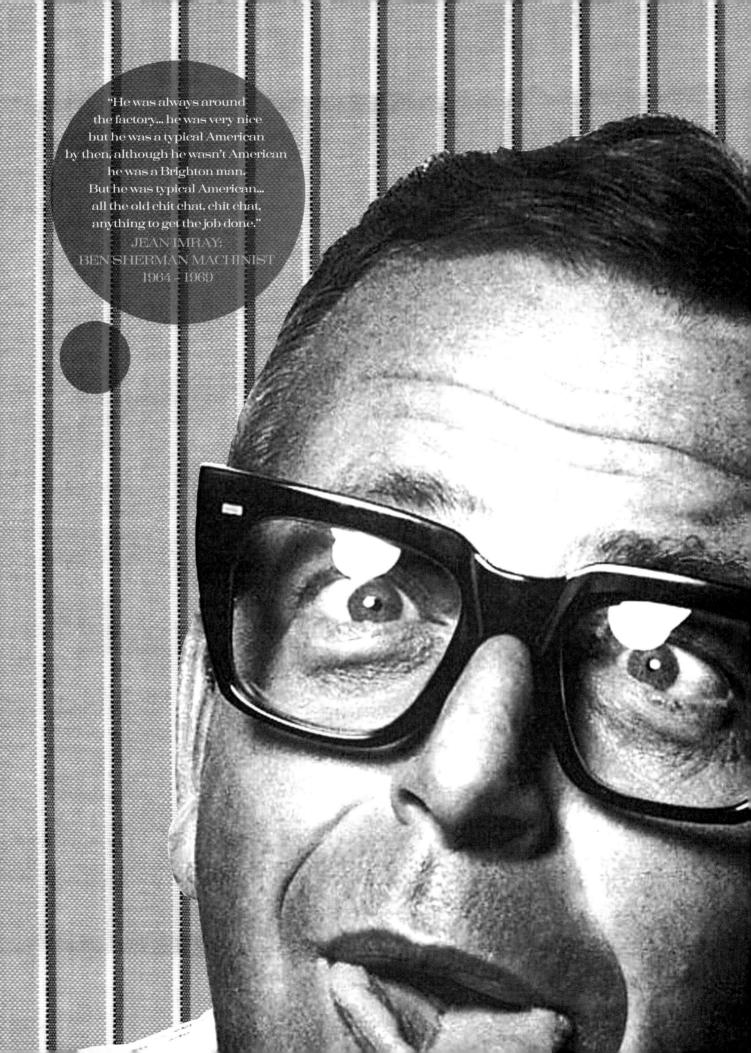

"He was always around
the factory... he was very nice
but he was a typical American
by then, although he wasn't American
he was a Brighton man.
But he was typical American...
all the old chit chat, chit chat,
anything to get the job done."

JEAN IMRAY:
BEN SHERMAN MACHINIST
1964 – 1969

At the same time, Arthur applied for, and was given, American citizenship. He took this opportunity to change his name to Ben Sherman; Ben because that's what his family always called him, Sherman - as in the tank - was a good solid American name. For the rest of his life Ben would speak with a pronounced American accent.

One of Minken's business concerns was a shirt company named Lancia. It was here that Ben worked extensively. Yet despite the job security and the handsome financial rewards, he soon felt discontented.

He found the style of Lancia shirts too conservative and ached to bring in his own designs, his own ideas. Unable to do so, he was reduced to treading water, a condition he found intolerable. Sherman was a man who always embraced the new and the different.

"We lived on Tampa Avenue," his son Martin recalls, "and my father brought home our first colour TV set. We were the first on the block to own one. That was very like my

father. He liked having fine things. He would always search for the best. He hated regular things that everyone else had. Not that he wanted to be 'better' but he loved the special aspect of searching out things that were unavailable to those who couldn't see what was there."

Ben's passion for independent thought and action informed much of Martin's childhood. He states that his father's words have proved of great worth to him in later life.

"He would always say things like 'anyone could have that' or 'anyone could have made one of those', or 'anyone could have figured that out'," Martin recalls, "In fact, when he wanted to berate you, he would say, 'do you realise that anybody could have done that?' That was the worst thing you wanted to hear from him. I remember getting into trouble with him and he told me, 'continue like that and you will end up exactly like everyone else.' He was so upset with me for not thinking about what I did, that I hadn't ensured the result was a special result and not just the regular answer everyone else could come up with."

Bored and frustrated at Lancia, news reached Ben that his mother was seriously ill. He quit his secure job and persuaded Ruth to relocate the family back to England.

To support him in his new venture, Ruth sold her shares in her father's swimwear business and in 1962 the Sherman family came back to Brighton.

"He bought the entire Lancia collection with him," Bill Knightsbridge, a key player in the Ben Sherman story, recalled. "It was a huge amount of goods, everything from clip-on ties, that sort of sportswear they call cruise-wear and shirts, long sleeved shirts, tab collar shirts, button-down shirts, Oxford shirts, everything you could imagine. There were no trousers, no outer clothes, just shirts, ties and cruise wear. It was astonishing merchandise."

The family stayed at Ben's parent's house in Palmeira Place, Hove. A third son, James, was born but marital problems were now

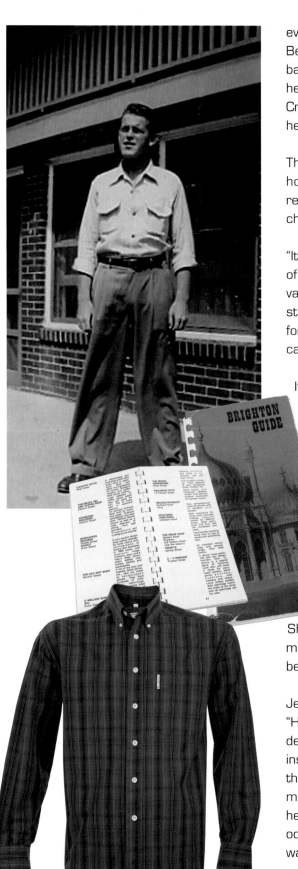

evident. As a solution, it was decided that Ben would stay in Britain while family went back to Los Angeles. A year later, Ruth and her sons returned to live in a flat in Furze Croft, Brighton but the marriage did not heal itself.

The family returned to the States, but Ben, however, did not shirk his family responsibilities. He would always visit his children at least two or three times a year.

"It was usually all quality time," Martin says of these visits. "There was Disneyland, vacations, dinners, shopping. He liked to stay abreast of our lives, he never let us forget we had a father and that we could call if we needed anything."

If he was unsuccessful within the confines of matrimony, Ben's business career certainly showed no signs of defeat. His first major move was to rent a factory in Bedford Square, Brighton, from a bankrupt businessman named Geofrey Saffier (Sherman took over Saffier's lease).

Ironically, the Saffier family had once run a massive shirt empire from these premises but had gone out of business. Ben Sherman took their place and began manufacturing a wide range of shirts and beachwear.

Jean Imray, an early employee, recalls, "He used to make towelling jackets, cotton denim on the outside and towelling on the inside for beachwear. But shirts were the thing. When I first started there he was making shirts for other companies and then he slowly, very slowly started to introduce odd samples and bits and pieces that he wanted to do. That's how it all started."

"Before we started having all our stagewear made, we wore Ben Sherman button-downs and we used to customise them - we'd sew army stripes and patches on the sleeves, and add epaulettes to the shoulders. We had a saying that our music was 'red with purple flashes', and to back that up I wore a bright red shirt with white buttons. It looked great up on stage behind the red Gibson 335."

EDDIE PHILLIPS:
THE CREATION

THE CREATION. FROM TOP: EDDIE PHILLIPS, JACK JONES, KENNY PICKETT, BOB GARNER

The company made other items; swimming trunks in printed cotton with matching half sleeve shirts, printed corduroy shirts plus a snap tatch shirt with interchangeable collars, a real innovation for the time. Then came tab collar shirts in bright pinks and blue followed by shirts with Giraffe collars and long pointed collars.

Initially, Ben's intended clientele were the well-to-do, those rich enough to holiday several times a year. Which is how Ronnie Wiseman entered Sherman's life.

Wiseman was an East London boy, who like many from his part of town had entered the rag trade at an early age.

"He had established a market," says Bill Knightsbridge, "in what is now called 'classy menswear'. He had customers who went on cruises, went to Bermuda and places like that and so created a market for that sort of exotic beachwear."

One day, a client of Ronnie's named Davy Collins, suggested he should meet Ben Sherman as both men had a lot in common. The next day, Wiseman travelled down to Brighton. Collins was right.

"We hit it off straight away," Wiseman recalls. "Ben gave me a small collection of beachwear and I went away. He called me soon after, asked me what had happened. I said, 'I've opened three accounts.' He nearly went through the roof! He said, 'Come down again. I'll pay the train fare.'"

Ben offered Ronnie a position in the company: chief salesman. Ronnie said he wasn't sure. He was making good money already. Ben asked how much he made in a year. Ronnie gave him the number. Ben's reply was simple. "I'll give you fifty per cent more." And he did.

"It's very hard to put your finger on it," Wiseman says, "but sometimes two people meet and they gel straight away. We got on like a house on fire, we were very, very close yet on the surface we shouldn't have been. I was into every sport and he had no sports interest at all. I played golf, cricket, football but Ben wasn't interested at all. We did have the same taste in music, which was jazz, but what we really had in common was that we enjoyed business. We enjoyed working together. We got a great kick from buying fabrics that turned into winners."

Having failed his daughter in marriage, Aaron Minken insisted Sherman stop trading under the Lancia name. Sherman complied and came up with the name, Sussex Shirts. This worked in the interim but in truth it was far too parochial a title.

Sherman then suggested to Wiseman they personalise the business by using either one of their names. (In 1959, Pierre Cardin had shocked the world of couture by launching his own Pierre Cardin – Paris label in shops, thus creating the first ever designer label. The creator's name as logo was now standard practice.)

"Ben said, 'We'll toss a coin and whoever wins, that's the name we'll use'," Wiseman reveals. "We tossed a coin. I won. Ben said, 'Let's make it best of three.'"

Two tosses of the coin later and the Ben Sherman company was born.

It arrived at a fortuitous time. British menswear was in the first throes of a major revolution. Prior to the Second World War the fashion world was simple: men mainly wore suits, women wore fashion. In the late 40s, that all changed. A group of upper class men began dressing in a neo-Edwardian style that in the mid-50s was appropriated by a group of young working class men who called themselves the Teddy Boys.

Major department stores of the time did not cater to this group or indeed to a wider male audience. Their neglect left a gap which others were quick to fill. One of these

"Before Ben Sherman came along,
shirts were just shirts. Suddenly you
could go to a clothes shop and ask for a
shirt by the brand name and each one was
individual, all sorts of colours and patterns,
but I always, always went for the checks.
I used to drive my mother mad badgering
her to make sure at least one was washed,
ironed and ready to wear every weekend."
KEN BROWNE,
ORIGINAL BRIGHTON MOD
1965

was a shop called Vince, situated off Carnaby Street. Although the shop's clientele may have been gay their fashions intrigued many. One such case was the young Glaswegian tailor, John Stephen, who was very much taken with Vince's collection of lime green underpants and skimpy swimwear. He worked at the shop and suitably inspired, later began creating colourful clothes for the colourful young. Stephen opened up his first shop in Beak Street before later moving onto Carnaby Street, then a dingy little street with no glamour to light its dark buildings.

Colour was something that intrigued Ben Sherman as well. He liked the button down shirts he had been selling in America but firmly believed he could improve on them by introducing a different design, brighter colours and other fabrics. He also wanted to go against the grain and put each shirt in an individual box.

Jack Lyons, a family member through marriage, recalls, "You used to get brown cardboard boxes with a dozen shirts in, all size fifteen, fifteen and a half, sixteen, 'cos that's the way the shops sold them. You took them out to show people. But Ben had this idea… see, Ben had the gift of the gab, he could talk you into things. But he also had wonderful ideas and I think he got most of them in America, that kind of salesmanship and presentation thing."

Despite the exorbitant price demanded for imported American shirts by shops such as Austins on Shaftesbury Avenue, the shirts were finding big favour with a young,

working class audience. Sherman's skill was to provide them with a cheaper, high quality replacement.

Phil Labatto, who would later work with Ben, recalls shopping for a certain style of shirt in Austins in the early 60s.

"They didn't have it so I went up to Cecil Gee and they didn't have them either, but they did say if you go up the road there's a shop (and you couldn't open a shop with this name again) called Gaylord and in the window you'll see a Ben Sherman. I went up there, checked it out. It looked good, so I bought it."

"There was this tremendous upsurge in fashion," Bill Knightsbridge recalls, "and Ben was willing to go along with it."

This new group of youngsters had a name - they called themselves the Modernists.

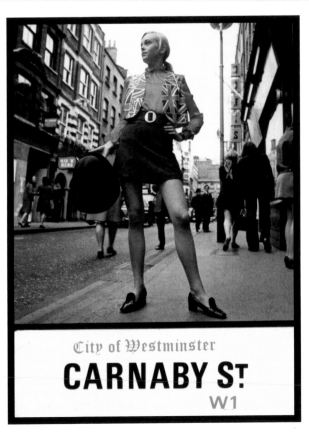

City of Westminster
CARNABY ST.
W.1

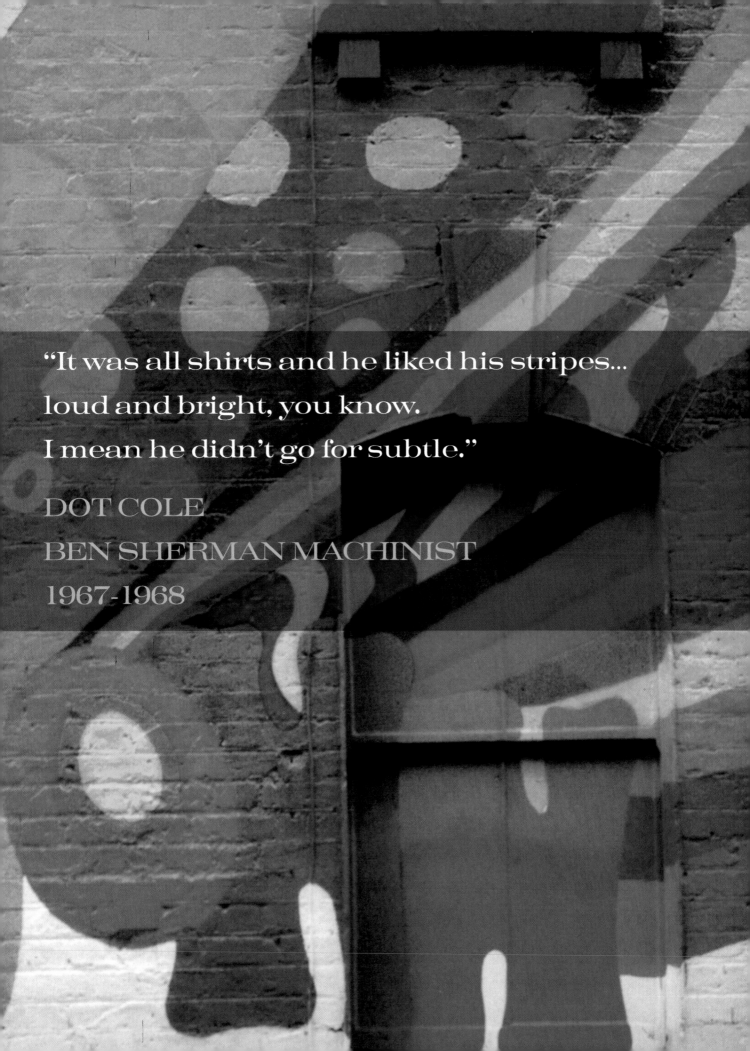

"It was all shirts and he liked his stripes...
loud and bright, you know.
I mean he didn't go for subtle."

DOT COLE
BEN SHERMAN MACHINIST
1967-1968

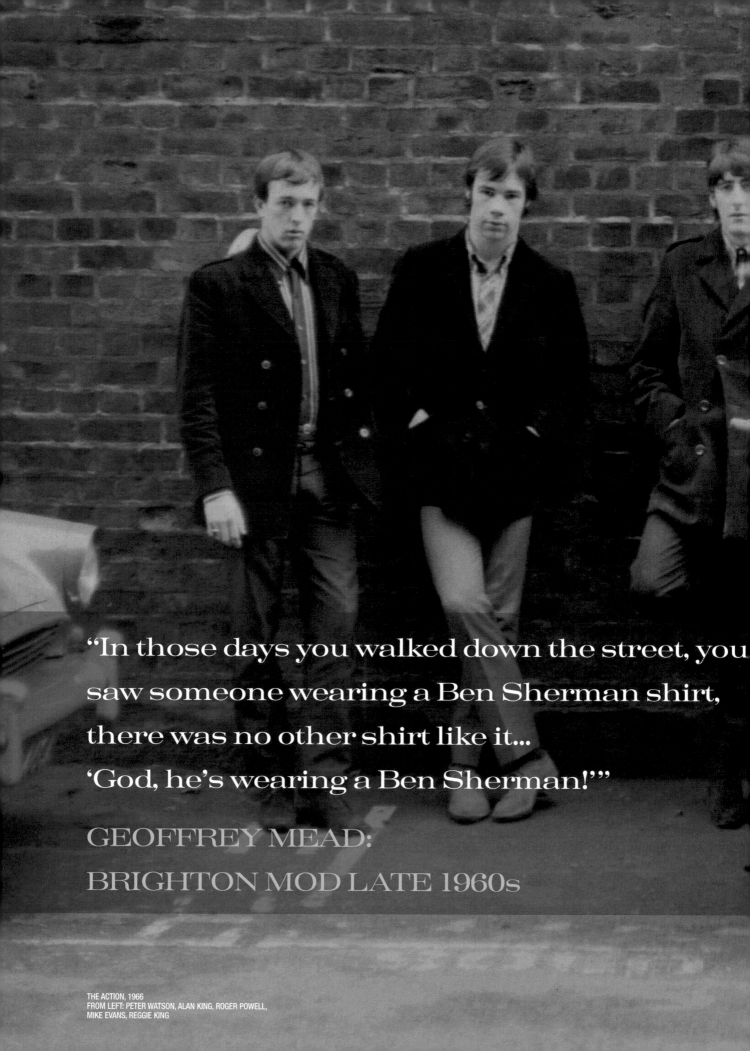

"In those days you walked down the street, you saw someone wearing a Ben Sherman shirt, there was no other shirt like it... 'God, he's wearing a Ben Sherman!'"

GEOFFREY MEAD:
BRIGHTON MOD LATE 1960s

THE ACTION, 1966
FROM LEFT: PETER WATSON, ALAN KING, ROGER POWELL,
MIKE EVANS, REGGIE KING

IN MOD WE TRUST...

"I had a phone call
from Lord John, saying Ronnie
Lane wanted to buy some shirts...
All of them! We had 100 delivered,
piled up in the corner of the office.
Ronnie couldn't have someone
wearing the same shirt as him."
TONY CALDER:
SMALL FACES
MANAGEMENT

"In the 60s I used to go down Carnaby Street for my shirts and my first and favourite Ben Sherman was a bright orange button-down. In fact I've still got a Ben Sherman collection from the Mod days - never been worn and still their packaging - fantastic wild colours - yello and purples. Beautiful."

CHRIS FARLOWE: SINGER

By the time the skinheads were identified as a new and separate group of teenage trouble makers, youth cults, or youth styles, had become a part of every British kids' rite of passage.

The year was 1968 when this particular and very distinctive group emerged, a continuation of previous trends but a fully formed and self-sufficient entity nonetheless.

The Teddy Boys of the late 50s had started the tribal ball rolling with their highly conspicuous uniform of Edwardian drape coats, drainpipe trousers and brightly coloured brothel creeper shoes.

They even had their own hairstyle, which was a curious combination of a painstakingly coiffured trunk at the front, (a quiff) and what appeared to be perfect replica of a duck's arse at the back (the DA).

Both were greased into shape with the help of copious handfuls of Brylcreem and left to set. The Teds distanced themselves from the normal and conventional strands of society by revelling in antisocial behaviour, which was punctuated by random acts of violence. They loved rock and roll of the Razzle Dazzle, Tutti Frutti variety, danced in cinema aisles and dated girls with hairdos that looked like your mother's.

OK, granted, all of that we know, but just how did such characters appear on the streets of a grey post war Britain in the 1950s. And just how did they manage to kick-start a cultural revolution that spawned every parent's nightmare; namely....

THE TEENAGER!

NO NO NO! Don't lose heart, I'll be brief, because I know more nonsense has been written about the birth of rock and roll, and the 50s and 60s, than any other recent era. But then to be fair that's hardly surprising, as so many people really do remember them.

Specifically the 50s, which are often portrayed as a time when Britain made a conscious effort to embrace the Brave New World and forget about the Second World War for a while.

The problem with eras is they don't really have a hard and fast cut-off point. They sort of evolve into one another, a bit like the youth cults covered in this book.

Fifties England was obviously full of people who'd grown up during the war. They'd either fought in it, or at the very least survived it, and like all wars WW2 had been a 'right 'ole eye opener' for everyone.

For one, a lot of British people found themselves travelling abroad for the first time. They'd also experienced things they'd never believed possible, be it legal or otherwise and lived through a time that had brought immense loss and tragedy, yet immeasurable unity and joy, plus - and let it be said - immense excitement.

In a word, they'd been 'changed' forever... and they knew it.

Aside from anything else, the British Army had dispensed over seventy million Benzedrine amphetamine tablets to its forces during the final stages of that war, which is not to say that the country was suddenly full of newly demobbed speed freaks, just that there were enough ex-servicemen wired by chemically fuelled adrenaline to make a difference to the old place.

"This was my Cleopatra phase when the Birds went sort of 'regency' mod. Clothes were really important to the band, especially me and Kim. We used to customise a lot of our clothes, like sticking that black and white checkered tape you put on cars on our belts and our guitars. Everywhere. We all had some great shirts at this time. Ben Shermans. The brighter the better."

RON WOOD:
THE BIRDS

"Ben Sherman was all I ever used to wear. I used to get them from Lord John in Carnaby Street as soon as they came out. I was lucky... 'cos I was in a band our manager would get them as freebies for promotion purposes. My first all-time fave was a brilliant white one with lots of multicoloured stripes. Another top fave was a beautiful dark green one with maroon stripes, yeah... I was big on stripes. In our scene back then, a BS as a fashion statement was very important, and bloody important to me for stagewear. They were, and still are, my favourite shirt."

ALI McKENZIE :
THE BIRDS

"It was the Mod days, nice clothes were half the battle... I lived out of the dustbins on the back streets of Carnaby. Carnaby Street was actually, at one time, quite fashionable, before it became known to everybody in London. The very best young designers were down there and because they were very expensive Italians, if any of the shirts had a button off the collar or anything like that, it would go in the dustbin. Me and Marc Bolan would go around at night and nick all the stuff out of the dustbins. Entire wardrobes of clothes for, well, nothing. All you had to do was sew a button on or stitch a sleeve. I remember when I used to steal everything. Had to look fashionable."

DAVID BOWIE: INTERVIEW

Not surprising then, they'd learnt to see things a little differently, and therefore reacted accordingly. True, there were those who wanted to settle back into the old cap doffing ways, of pre-war Blighty, where the finer things in life were considered a nice cup of tea, a Saturday night fumble with the wife (if they were lucky) followed by a Woodbine.

But not everyone was going to settle for that. For now there were young men the length and breadth of the country wanting to be like Lawrence Harvey's character Joe Lampton in the film *Room At the Top*. Independent and forward thinking.

Women too, many who'd had independence forced upon them were now equally self sufficient, working in factories and living single lives. These people found they liked this new life and they had no intention of giving it up.

Social subversives all of them, and nothing spreads as fast as a new idea. The compulsory call up had been abolished for boys of eighteen and the younger population as a whole was growing edgy, which may partly explain the hard sell of bedtime drinks

like Horlicks, and BournVita, both strong smelling and tasting concoctions that promised the sort of sound sleep which would lead to contentment, success and a new three piece suite.

No, these people were hip to it. They'd had their fill of government information films representing ideals, propaganda or just plain wishful thinking. They didn't want to settle for what had gone before. Social mobility was in the air.

The consumer had just been granted hire purchase while discovering G-Plan furniture. The working class could now afford TV sets, drip-dry shirts, and in some cases even a car. The advertisers were most importantly telling people how to deal with body odour and the government told one and all that they'd never had it so good.

The public mood was ripe for change and on the look out for that continuation of excitement, Basically it all added up to the fact that England was ready to rock and roll. However what it doesn't explain is the unlikely way in which it arrived.

The first truly bona fide rock and roll star was a man whose music transformed literally millions of young adults into what we now know the world over as teenagers. His name was Bill Haley and he was almost thirty when he first burst into the public's consciousness. He was also fat, married with five kids and sported the sort of comical haircut that to my knowledge has never been repeated.

Yet he single handedly sparked the first revolt by a younger generation against its elders. He had his first hit 'Crazy Man Crazy' in 1953 which was a song that's now acknowledged as the very first rock and roll record to ever enter a national chart. He then followed that a whole year later with the classic 'Shake Rattle And Roll', a record that saw the portly rocker spend a unprecedented twelve weeks at number one. Then he got REALLY popular.

Haley's third single, a novelty foxtrot, entitled 'Rock Around The Clock' was played behind the opening credits of *The Blackboard Jungle* (another first) a film about a beleaguered black teacher's struggle to gain the respect of his students in a run-down slum school.

Juvenile delinquency and rock and roll proved to be an irresistible recipe and the film provided another significant first for Haley. *The Blackboard Jungle* was the first time rock music was featured in a movie score.

Haley was promptly snapped up by Columbia Pictures and starred in his own movie *Rock Around The Clock*. Suddenly Haley was the biggest recording artist in the world.

When *The Blackboard Jungle* opened in the UK it caused a seat-slashing frenzy in cinemas everywhere as Teddy Boys ran wild in the aisles. It was the first real tabloid mention of Teddy Boy terror and Haley hysteria. It was also effectively the last. For once Haley hit Britain in person, it was

"The Action were a very
fashion conscious band. A lot
of mods would come to see us
play live to check out what we
were wearing... what kind of button-down
shirts we had on or what cut of trousers.
We were always up and down Carnaby
Street 'cos our manager had set up
an expense account with the best shops,
and Ben Sherman were always
a big favourite."

MIKE EVANS :
THE ACTION

Evening Argus

Monday
May 18, 1964

Incorporating the
SUSSEX DAILY NEWS

3d.

NIGHT EXTRA

Mods let fly at the Rockers in fierce seafront clashes

BATTLE OF BRIGHTON

Fifty arrested

ABOUT 50 teenagers were arrested today after fierce clashes on Brighton seafront between police and Mods and Rockers. Hundreds of holidaymakers gathered outside the police station as the teenagers were bundled out of police vans.

Police took possession of a number of weapons, including studded belts, an airgun and a golf club.

Trouble started soon after 9.30 a.m., when several hundred Mods went Rocker-hunting, armed with stones from the beach.

As scores of white-helmeted police arrived in radio-controlled vans there were scenes reminiscent of race riots. Teenagers yelled: "Get stones from the beach." One was hurled through the window of a squad car.

As police in plain clothes and a mounted policeman attempted to break up crowds, teenagers began jeering and fighting broke out. An empty bottle was hurled at the head of the police horse, but rider P.C. Ken Thomas deflected it with his hand.

A tidal wave of shouting youths knocked people from the pavements as they swept down from

DEATH OF A MOD

A 17-YEAR-OLD youth who rode his new scooter to Brighton with more than 30 Mods fell to his death from the 100ft.-high cliffs at Saltdean early today. He had been sleeping out with friends on the cliff top.

FULL STORY: PAGE 8

the West Pier to congregate at the Palace Pier.

An old lady with a young child burst into hysterical crying as the jostling mass swept past her. She stood helpless until people working in seafront stalls came to her rescue and calmed her down.

Elderly holidaymakers fled from the seafront to avoid the crowds of hysterical teenagers.

A screaming mob of 200 teenagers chased a young boy across

the beaches, hurling stones as they ran. Police moved in and rescued the boy, who was later taken to hospital suffering from a leg injury. Police later said he was only 13 years old.

Police reinforcements from East Sussex, West Sussex and Hastings were brought in, bringing the number of policemen on duty to about 150.

Many of the Brighton policemen had been on duty for more than 14 hours yesterday and returned to the scene this morning after only a few hours' sleep. At the height of the battles the crowd numbered between 2,000 and 3,000.

Gradually police herded the teenagers past the Palace Pier and along Madeira Drive, but several hundred Mods broke away and rushed on to the Aquarium Sun Terrace.

ROCKERS JUMP

They cornered a dozen Rockers and started pelting them with deckchairs.

The outnumbered Rockers escaped by jumping 20ft. from the terrace into the arms of the waiting police. Several were bundled into police cars.

Then Rockers on motor-cycles ran the gauntlet of litter-throwing Mods who lined the railings of the raised terraces. A metal basket dropped from more that narrowly missed one youth

While uniformed police set up the crowds plainclothes men stopped teenagers and searched their bedrolls for weapons.

To move men to police commandeered trolled Civil Defence tion vans.

Shortly before and Rockers Palace Pier and jeering as police tr

The poli worked along men as the l stage a mas promenade.

POLICE IT

A policeman red wh

The deckchair battle in progress at the Aquarium

promenade near the Mermaid Pavilion Restaurant. Five girls were later taken in the an ambulance. A large contingent of police were called to restore order.

A senior police officer said that trouble started when somebody threw a stone at the ambulance which was waiting to take away a holidaymaker injured on the beach earlier.

ONLOOKERS

One woman onlooker commented: "They all ought to be put in jail—an old-fashioned jail. They are all a nasty, dirty, stinking lot. The police much more to do be-sid offer a lot of silly te

senior police officer agreed er that the force's job was icated by the large crowds olidaymakers who congregated ise trouble seemed to be

called to the White at Rottingdean this r a group of youths ken bottle into the k. Several teenagers o Rottingdean police

manager, Mr Ray "The law were d the more taken

CLAC ION EASI TE WHILE GE COURT W GES: PA 7

TWO STABBED IN MARGATE FLARE-UP

Police rout marching Mods

AS further trouble flared up today between Mods and Rockers at Margate two youths were taken to hospital with stab wounds. Later while the magistrates were hearing 51 cases at the town hall, a crowd of 200 Mods march there chanting: "Come u Rockers."

A lice er and three other rs n them and the inspec ard Break them up."

As advanced, the Mods s all directions.

An ove in the railway stat which was packed wi ne started a cafe battle Mods at breakfast tim

Mrs. Li Sto e manageress, who was n to floor, said: "The b at it was so good lou used. you

up s with the i sh show off t

Stott yout!

The

ty-one y the two 39 of using ne of be posse offensive ons, inclu parts of deck-airs, knives and a cosh; two of wilful damage to deckchairs and a plate-glass window; one of incit breach of the peace; and one assault on the police.

Most of the youths come from ndon and from Kent towns.

SEE "THUGS" SENTEN **PAGE 8**

17 more die on roads

SEVENTEEN people were killed in accidents on Britain's roads yesterday, according to provisional figures issued in London today by the Ministry of Transport.

It brings the provisional total for the first three days of the Whitsun holiday 7.

ight people accidents hit Sunde t year, when y at th e stage of the

liament inistry of Trans awards at the Racing Club's 1 00 the bi iate casualty

people mposs to me ad tor or lying f in pital. Do d let it he

E R

Twenty-s cour

Twen ven youths them fr the Londo ppeared efe a specia group in del another among the fight v whist the ght of th the of the M and kir the runni

The charges cluded possessing weap of steal o of th of th

ny periods

ay 5.18 p.m 6.29 p m
Sea temperature 56 degrees.
Lights: 9.20 p m to 1.32

Mar bea warmes peratue in 23c (73F). At one of the

painfully obvious that this overweight, perspiring cowboy in a garish tartan jacket wasn't the rebel icon Britain's youth had been expecting!

Elvis, Chuck Berry, Little Richard and the like were waiting in the wings to encourage youth to rock on for a few more years. Yet as the 50s drew to a close the whole Ted phenomenon, like some lost Tibetan tribe, inexplicably faded away. They have of course made the odd reappearance throughout the years, most noticeably in the late 70s.

The Teds were succeeded by the new kids on the rock block, 'The Mods' and their cultural counterparts 'The Rockers'.

In addition there were Beatniks, Spivs and Trad Jazzers, all blurring the edges of this transitional period. However they never managed to capture the media's attention in quite the same way. Consequently each successive generation of teenage cults initially strived to establish itself independently from the previous one.

However, some elements were almost inevitably passed on. The Mods admittedly borrowed little from the Teds but they did recognise their love of colour and flair.

Before the Teds, clothes in the UK were basically a necessity. They were ordinary, unflattering and practical. The Teds changed all that by showing how clothes could be individual and fun. They broke new ground and in turn established the teenage market. They also made it acceptable for males to dress for no other reason than to stand out in a crowd. It was a liberationist and individualist attitude that suited the Mods down to the ground. The paradoxical problem that followed, however (and one that all the so called 'outsider' cults suffer from), is that in trying to be different they inevitably have to conform and accept some type of uniform. Then, and only then, could they proclaim their individuality and identity.

Even the Mods, who recognised this better than anyone by constantly evolving, were eventually consumed by high street commercialism and mass-market production.

Mods were seen in and around the Soho area of London as early as 1959, never in large numbers but distinguishable by their dark Italian suits and winkle picker shoes, which was the basic look that developed over the next two to three years.

Although widely considered as a working class movement the originators were mostly from a white middle class background, predominantly Jewish and with connections in the rag trade. It was a very male dominated movement, totally clothes-obsessed and incredibly vain. The first Mods were quite isolated individuals existing independently of one another, yet pursuing a common interest and passion. They were also heavily into modern jazz as opposed to the traditional version beloved by the beatniks and trad-jazzers. In fact it was because of their modern jazz tastes that they called themselves Modernists.

Although few in number, these early Mods were noticed and talked about and eventually imitated by others. Slowly their influence spread and the Italian look evolved. Most suits were still bought off the peg but the Mods would make small tailored changes to them, making each one slightly individual. Eventually they started to have suits made, thanks mainly to the 'Hire Purchase' (HP) instalment payment scheme.

Trousers were narrow at first but varied between 14" and 16" bottoms. There was a short period of bell bottoms and even stepped bottoms, which meant a cut away at the front which sat on top of the shoe and a longer back which covered the heel.

They could also be finished off with little slits at the side or have buttons running up the seam. The suits were nearly always dark blue and black, pin striped or plain, although herringbone and Prince of Wales check were also popular for a time.

ALFREDO MARCANTONIO - ITALY c1966.
NOTE THE HIGHLY SOUGHT AFTER LARGE FACED CHRONO WATCH!

"As early Modernists we had this incredible obsession with minutae: the way Belmondo smoked his Gitane in 'Au bout de Souffle', the need for the original recording of a song on the original label, the fine but often functionless detailing on a piece of clothing. This is where the Ben Sherman came into its own. The soft roll collar with its tiny buttons and equally miniature, perfectly stitched buttonholes. The back with its central box pleat and neatly tailored 'hanging' loop. The vivid stripes and pastel colours. These things set you apart and placed you above other men. The cool, classic, stylish button-down became more accessible and more affordable. Ben Sherman was the Henry Ford of the shirt world."

ALFREDO MARCANTONIO:
1960s MOD

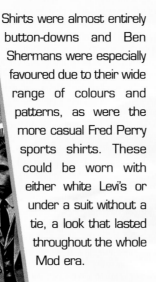

Shirts were almost entirely button-downs and Ben Shermans were especially favoured due to their wide range of colours and patterns, as were the more casual Fred Perry sports shirts. These could be worn with either white Levi's or under a suit without a tie, a look that lasted throughout the whole Mod era.

The Italian and French haircuts came in around 1960 and were always finished dry as opposed to the accepted oiled and greased look. This in itself was something of a breakthrough, for up until then British barbers had simply cut men's hair for purely practical reasons and never for style, so naturally prices rose accordingly.

It wasn't just continental hairstyles that the Mods adopted either. Anything Italian was in and anything French was considered the ultimate in cool. So cool in fact that Mods

would spend hours studying classic black and white French films like *Shoot The Pianist* staring Charles Aznavour or mimed nonsense like *Yo Yo* with Marcel Marceau, whose black and white hooped pullover was a much desired item. The big hero was Jean Paul Belmondo. Cigarettes had to be Gitanes or Gauloise and girlfriends had to look like Jean Seberg, although that was probably a taller order than simply buying French fags!

Probably the most enduring image associated with Mod, even at this early stage, was the scooter. Lambretta or Vespa, depending on your preference. The rider wore a parka, which were US army khaki coloured all-weather anoraks. These protected the rider's clothes and were stored in a front or rear rack on the bike.

Although the basic Mod look was well established by 1961, there was still no common sense of identity on a large scale. This was mainly due to the fact that the media had yet to discover them.

That all changed in 1962 when the magazine *Town* ran a feature on a group of hip young things from Stamford Hill. One of those kids was fifteen-year-old Mark Feld, who later emerged as Marc Bolan, the

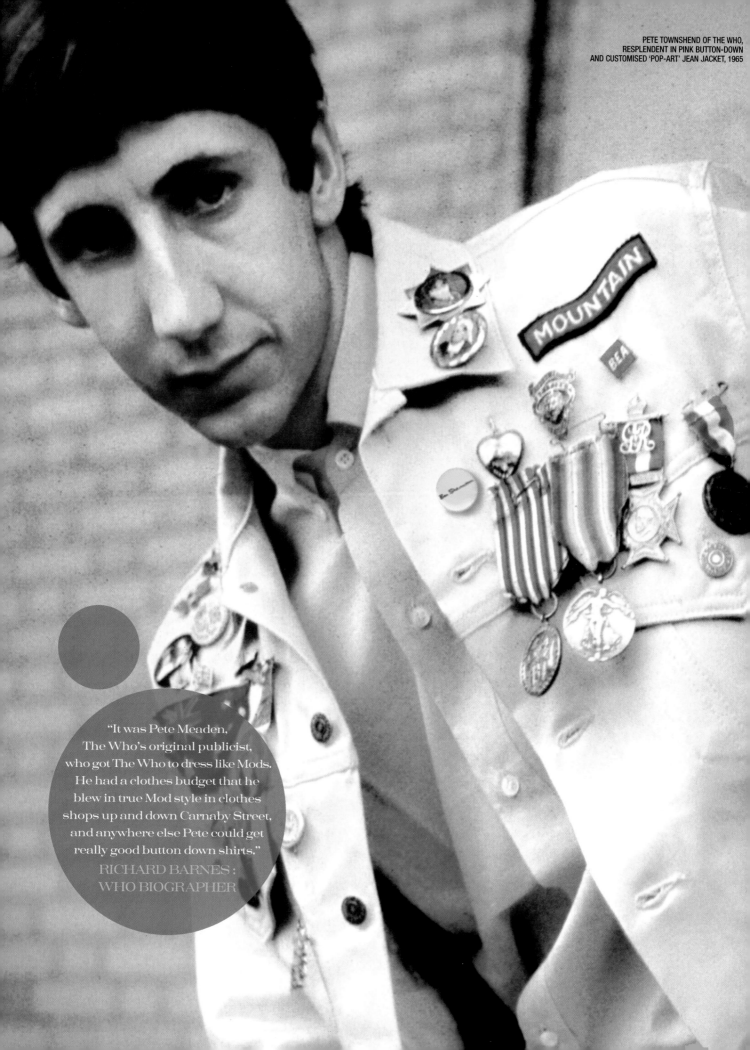

"It was Pete Meaden,
The Who's original publicist,
who got The Who to dress like Mods.
He had a clothes budget that he
blew in true Mod style in clothes
shops up and down Carnaby Street,
and anywhere else Pete could get
really good button down shirts."

RICHARD BARNES :
WHO BIOGRAPHER

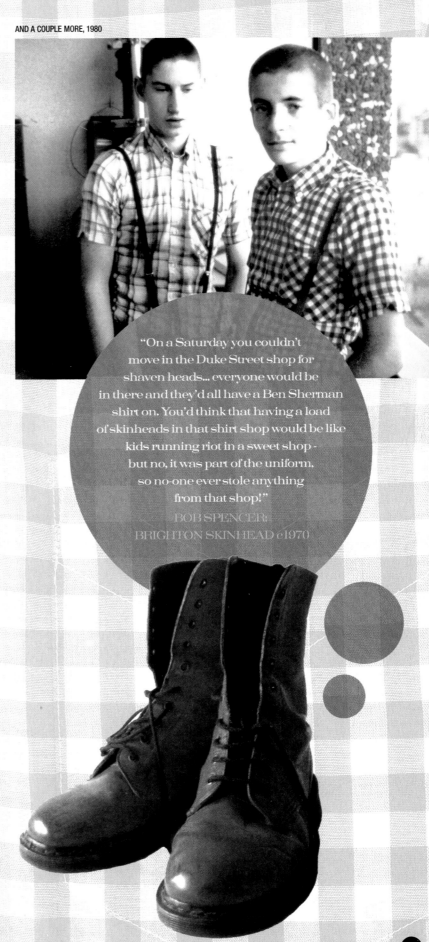

glittering pixie of glam rock. In the interview they talked about their attitude towards all things sartorial and moaned about the difficulty of finding good tailors and shoes. They also peppered their speak with slang buzzwords like 'faces' and 'tickets' and name checked shops such as John Stevens and John Michael.

It was only a small article, but it was the first media coverage these dedicated devotees of fashion had received and it opened the fashion floodgates. It was all the confirmation the little pockets of Mods needed to fuse together and cultivate a wider and distinctive movement.

From then on the Modernists became Mods and a very British phenomenon was born.

1964 and 1965 were the peak years for Mod. However, once the media had discovered them, the term Mod was literally applied to everything and everyone. Suddenly Mods had their own TV shows, magazines, clubs, clothes shops and pop groups, taking something that had started out elusive and exclusive and turning it into the mundane and mainstream.

"On a Saturday you couldn't move in the Duke Street shop for shaven heads... everyone would be in there and they'd all have a Ben Sherman shirt on. You'd think that having a load of skinheads in that shirt shop would be like kids running riot in a sweet shop - but no, it was part of the uniform, so no-one ever stole anything from that shop!"

BOB SPENCER: BRIGHTON SKINHEAD c1970

"I was in my early twenties in art school, and I used to go into the 'fashion' classes - 'cos that's where the girls were! That was in my rebellious time, so I wore my first Ben Sherman shirt with my blue jeans to counter balance the look that I wanted. It was a pure white button-down. Classic. I carried this on in The Animals - we were very fashionable at the time - we played a very authentic R&B, so Mods were always in the audience. To them our clothes were as important as what we were playing. That dark suit and pastel button-down look was widely adopted."

ERIC BURDON:
THE ANIMALS

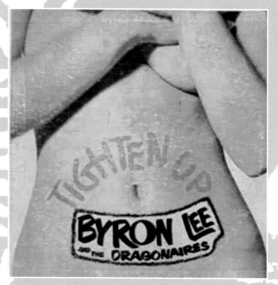

In April 1964 the first Mods - Rockers clash occured at the seaside. This only served to tarnish the Mod image even further and attracted a scruffier element that the editorials referred to as 'vermin low-life' and 'show-offs'.

Naturally the original movers and shakers of the movement wanted nothing to do with such tawdriness and the scene fractured in two with the earliest innovators dissociating themselves from the high street hooligan element and renaming themselves 'Stylists'. By 1967 a large proportion of these had leaned towards the Regency style foppery look best associated with the psychedelic era. This in turn progressed, with the help of LSD and some pretty extensive pot smoking, into the hippie look.

The other faction, harder and mainly working class, were equally affronted by what they saw as 'freaky frippery' and duly declared them their new adversaries. Anything that was considered even slightly effeminate was totally rejected in favour of a look that was unmistakably masculine. Clothes had to be hard wearing yet neat, practical yet smart. Or in other words, clothes that would stand up to the rigours of a fight, stay pressed and identify the wearer on a crowded football terrace.

The skinhead had arrived!

"Like a lot of the 60s
bands we started wearing
Ben Sherman shirts because they
were really colourful. Before that, shirts
were either white or in dull, drab colours.
All of a sudden you could get multi-striped
button-downs, checked ones, even polka dot
ones, if I remember rightly - the best colours
were Ben Shermans though, especially
those checks and pastels... gorgeous.
Yes - an indispensable part of my
wardrobe, then and now."

ART WOOD
MUSICIAN & ARTIST

WOODS

elmer

"Button-downs?
I'm the only one in this shot
not wearing one... probably didn't
have a clean one, but I did like
a Ben Sherman. When I was in the
Artwoods I lived at Art and Ron Wood's
and their mum used to iron all my shirts.
Apparently I still owe her
two shillings and sixpence."
JON LORD:
THE ARTWOODS
& DEEP PURPLE

ADVERTISING YOU COULDN'T BUY

"The Ben Sherman,
that was the ultimate shirt.
Yeah. It was the shirt to wear, it was
the shirt to be seen in... If you didn't have a
Ben Sherman there was a bit of piss taking.
You'd get ribbed if you went and bought a
Brutus shirt - but it was, I dunno, I wouldn't
say inferior... just it was sort of like a copy of a
Ben Sherman so you used to get ribbed."
BOB SPENCER:
BRIGHTON SKINHEAD
c1970

Not a lot pf people know this, but Richard Allen was a pen name for the Canadian born author, James Moffatt. In fact it was his then publishers, the New English Library, who came up with his pseudonym, one of dozens he was to use over the years. When he died in November 1993, the literary world hardly noted his passing, which was incredible given the impact his novels had on kids growing up in 1970s Britain.

Two of his titles, *Skinhead* and *Suedehead* were actually million sellers when first published in 1970, and books like *Terrace Terrors* and *Boot Boys* sold by the hundreds of thousands, bringing central characters like Joe Hawkins to life in classrooms up and down the country.

James Moffatt was neither a skinhead nor a suedehead, or anything else for that matter. He was in his forties when he wrote what are widely regarded as the ultimate in youth cult paperbacks.

However, Moffatt was most certainly a skinhead at heart, and he researched the cult with a love and respect for the subject. It was a love and respect that was obviously reciprocated too, for at the height of his fame he was receiving over a thousand fan letters a week. All from skinheads and other teenage tribes, turning him into a household name and earning Moffatt the reputation as one of the most prolific writers of his time.

During his writing career Moffatt produced over 400 titles, and wrote for countless magazines and newspapers. Yet he will be best remembered as the creator of the Richard Allen novels.

But what do we actually know about the man behind the regular sounding nom de plume? What inspired him to write such lurid and insightful tomes about punch-ups and piss-ups?

Well, it might have had something to do with his father. Apparently James Moffatt Snr was also a well known author and was famous for his book *King George Was My Shipmate*, a salty account of a life on the ocean waves with the future King of England, George VI.

The Moffatts may have hailed from Canada, but their origins were of Irish and Scottish descent, Celtic roots they were fiercely proud of. James Jnr was a well educated man, studying law and then chemistry at Queens University in Eastern Canada. However, his first love was writing and it was this and travel that consumed him for most of his life. Moffatt Jnr lived in New York for a number of years during the 1950s, churning out pot boilers before moving to Hollywood and becoming a publicist to the stars of the day.

From Hollywood he moved to Mexico and then Texas, where he became good friends with the fiery evangelist Billy Graham with whom he occasionally enjoyed a drink or two. After Texas it was back to Canada where he started his own magazine dedicated to the then booming sport of ten-pin bowling. Unfortunately a cheating partner forced the magazine to close, and Jim moved on to writing fiction, creating the character Johnny Canuck, a Canadian private dick who was part Philip Marlowe, and part Red Indian. Needless to say, Canuck always got his man and was especially successful with the ladies. The books were published by a Californian company, Leisure Books Inc, and were hugely popular.

Big Jim's motto was apparently, "enjoy today and tomorrow will take care of itself," and he believed it, living life large and to the full. He would often drive to Las Vegas to gamble,

badly, and in one night lost $8,000 - a lot of money in the 1950s! On one occasion, he even used his car as collateral for bets. He lost that too.

Moffatt was an established name by the time he arrived in Britain in 1961 and landed a job working with IPC and Compact Books. He also wrote freelance and penned many Christmas annuals for children as well as a number of picture strips for comics. His ability to turn his hand to almost any subject led to him hiding behind a string of nom de plumes - Anne North, Charles Saye, Etienne Aubin, Trudi Maxwell, Francis Duke, Johnny Douglas, Ron Cunningham, J. Kramer, Roger Blake, J.J. More, John London and, of course, Richard Allen.

It was under the guise of Richard Allen, while working a stint at New English Library, that Moffatt really hit his stride and found his niche. In an interview with *Skinhead Times* he explained how he stumbled upon the skinhead cult quite by chance.

"It was quite typical really. Some of my editors were having a party in London and one of them, a Chelsea fan, suggested a book about football aggro. My name was mentioned and since I had a reputation for being able to write faster than most others, he telephoned me. It was 10.30 at night and he explained the book was needed within a week. After some discussion I got a further three days for research. The next morning I drove to London's East End, where I believed an on-the-spot investigation would enlighten me about this relatively new cult. I found a pub which looked right for the job and, sure enough, some of the young drinkers were skinheads.

"They didn't like being questioned by strangers, but the moment I told them they were to be featured in a new book, they completely changed their attitude. They bought me beers and verbally fought for top-billing. And I had enough material to start typing!"

The result was *Skinhead* - the story of Joe Hawkins and his skinhead mates wreaking havoc at various London locations including an outdoor pop concert, lots of pubs and several football stadiums. Or, as the book's back cover blurb put it: "A book that portrays with horrifying vividness all the terror and brutality that has become the trademark of these vicious teenage malcontents."

It sold slowly for the first six months of its shelf life before picking up and eventually shifting well over a million copies. Which suggests there was either a million skinheads with their noses buried in their paperbacks, or there's something about the English that loves reading about random acts of violence. Whatever the reasons, the front cover artwork on *Skinhead* and many of Allen's subsequent novels brought Ben Sherman shirts into a million households and into the consciousness of a million impressionable teenagers. In an era where where there was no *Maxim, GQ* or *Loaded,* that's the sort of advertising you simply couldn't buy.

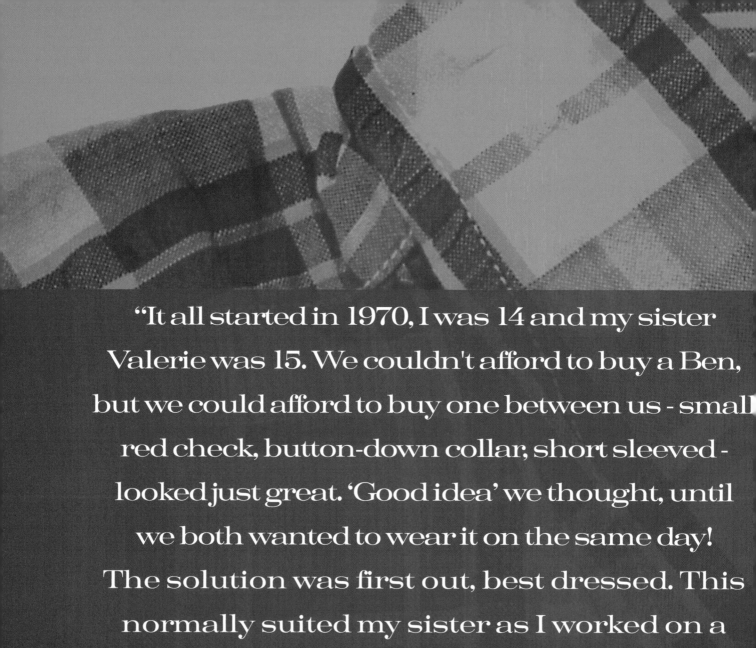

"It all started in 1970, I was 14 and my sister Valerie was 15. We couldn't afford to buy a Ben, but we could afford to buy one between us - small red check, button-down collar, short sleeved - looked just great. 'Good idea' we thought, until we both wanted to wear it on the same day! The solution was first out, best dressed. This normally suited my sister as I worked on a Saturday, so she would wear it all day.

Occasionally I would get my own back,
and I would hide Ben before I went to work.
Our mother, poor soul, spent most of her time
washing and ironing Ben, or denying that she
had seen who was wearing him that day.
What happened to Ben? I really don't know.
My sister left home before me and I bet she has
it hidden somewhere!"

PAUL 'HODGE' HODGSON

MILLIONS OF SHIRTS

GONE WEST... BEN SHERMAN WITH RONNIE WISEMAN SALES MANAGER, 1968

Ben Sherman was suited to business. He was tall, imposing. His height was 6'1, his weight, sixteen stone. He wore glasses and his temper was known to be quick, fearsome, yet he was also a lively, open man who worked non-stop to get his venture off the ground and handsomely rewarded those who showed similar belief. Unfortunately, this didn't include his family who thought his ideas terrible. Pale or bright coloured shirts for men wrapped in individual boxes? The colour pink used in a shirt? To them, Sherman's plans would cost him all he had. They gave him zero support.

"At the family shop," Daphne Sherman, his fourth wife recalls, "the staff wore white shirts with starched collars and a khaki overall. So Ben's ideas for pink, striped shirts, blue shirts, green shirts, just didn't make sense. 'Who's going to buy these shirts?' they would ask him. They all thought he was crazy."

Typically, Ben ignored them and forged ahead.

"At the beginning," Ronnie Wiseman says, "he was a workaholic. He would work seven days a week, from eight in the morning to eight at night. I can't remember anything he was obsessed with apart from work."

One of Ben's many strengths was an ability to employ suitable staff. Bill Knightsbridge was one. He went to Ben Sherman to learn the art of cutting and started off as an office boy.

"I was there to answer the telephone, dispatch goods," he recalls. "I ran the office and the warehouse and I certainly had no experience in doing either. Any spare time I could find I would be in the basement with the collection, trying things on, taking things out. Then this second factory came up at the clocktower and he took it on. It was a ladies swimwear factory and he started making the button-down shirts."

At first Sherman made shirts for shirt companies such as Rael Brooke but the work was standard, uninteresting. Ben couldn't help himself and gradually began inserting his own ideas into the mix until fairly soon, he was ready to launch his own shirt, the Ben Sherman.

The shirt was nothing if not eye catching. The button-down collars were big with a distinctive roll to them. The shirt front had a placket front (most shirts of the day did not) and a top left hand pocket. Later on, a black tag bearing Sherman's name in orange would be sewn onto the side of this pocket. Those unable to afford a Ben Sherman would be able to remove this tag and sew it onto their other 'inferior' shirts.

Unusually, a button had been placed in the middle of the back collar. Underneath the collar a long pleat with a small hook on the top ran down the shirt's back, two lines of stitching either side. To complement their style, the shirts were made in Oxford stripes in a wide variety of colours. Jean Imray recalls, "(Ben) had the Oxford cloth with all the lovely pale shades... pale pink, pale lemon, pale blue. And he did like a stripe."

It's basic design had been derived from the classic American Ivy League shirt but Ben's inventive touches - the hook, the button in the collar-and especially his use of colour and fabrics - created a distinctive clothing item.

"It did start as a copy of the American shirt," Ronnie Wiseman confirms, "but it turned into our own look. We put together this Ben Sherman range and we only used American fabrics. That meant that mothers loved washing the shirts because after they had been washed they looked brand new."

Wiseman was a good salesman. Soon after joining Ben he built up an impressive list of high class gentlemen's outfitters, keen to

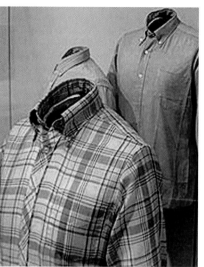

the company's range of dressing gowns, beachwear and formal shirts. But Wiseman was not content with just appealing to the wealthy. With the distinctive Ben Sherman shirts, he looked to other outlets, towards the young, many of whom were now gaining economic freedom and starting to make a name for themselves.

"I got an appointment with this guy who was all the rage at the time – John Stephen," Wiseman recalls. "He came to our showroom at about six in the evening. He got through a bottle of scotch and then put down an order which was astronomical. It was as much as we expected to do in the first year!"

Sensing the changing climate, the company deliberately started to move away from its original high-class clientele to concentrate its efforts elsewhere. The first town to capitulate was Newcastle.

"We had a customer up there that had two shops," Wiseman says. "I used to fly up and see him and come back with an order worth six or seven thousand pounds. All of a sudden another major company in Newcastle came onto us. I told them, 'I can't service you because it's impossible. We only have a limited production and these other people are taking thirty per cent of it.'"

Production lines were now increased at the Clocktower factory which was situated above a Burtons shop on the corner of West Street and North Street in Brighton. The building had three floors, one owned by a coat factory, the middle level belonging to Ben. The factory was accessed by a small anonymous doorway which led to an antiquated lift that creaked up to the second floor.

As the orders started mounting up, so the workforce started increasing. Twin sisters, Jean and Carol joined the company. So did Dorothy Cole.

TOP: RARE BEN SHERMANS FROM THE 2003 BRIGHTON EXHIBITION
MIDDLE: VINTAGE ADVERTISING BOTTTOM: THE BEN SHERMAN FACTORY GIRLS

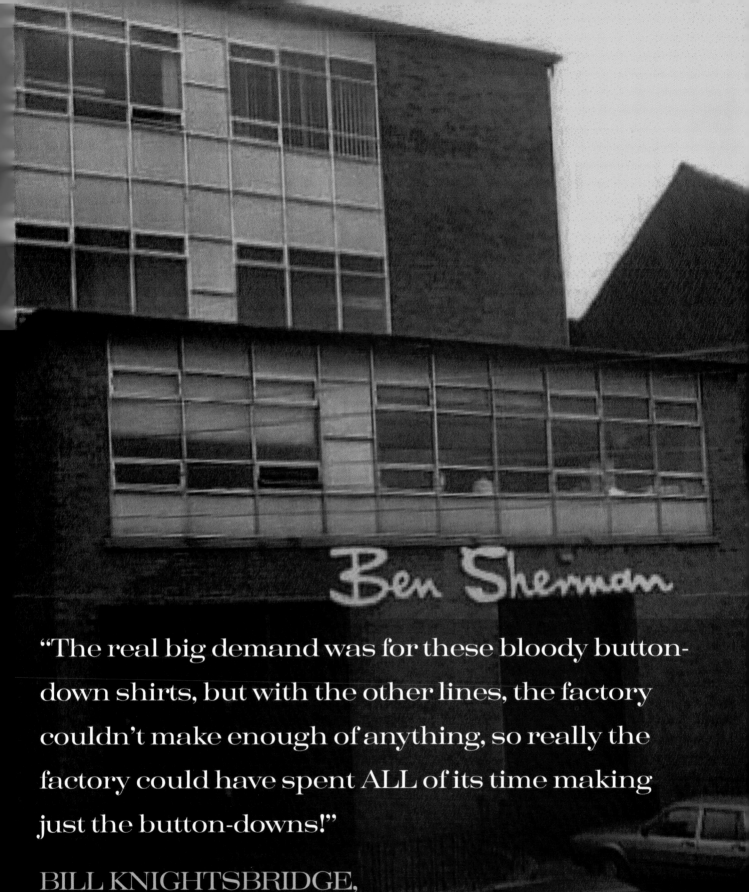

"The real big demand was for these bloody button-down shirts, but with the other lines, the factory couldn't make enough of anything, so really the factory could have spent ALL of its time making just the button-downs!"

BILL KNIGHTSBRIDGE,
EMPLOYEE OF BEN SHERMAN

"Our gang had an identity, we all wore Levi's with a precise turn up, which was, to quote my Dad 'at half mast', a pale blue T-shirt or a button down striped or checked Ben Sherman, or sometimes an Ivy League shirt with cufflinks, with maybe a cravat borrowed from our fathers' wardrobes, or a knitted slimline tie in a dark colour. This was all set off with either a jean jacket, a Harrington jacket or a safari jacket. The crowning glory was a pair of desert boots from Wood Green, or a pair of Italian shoes from Ravel in Carnaby Street.

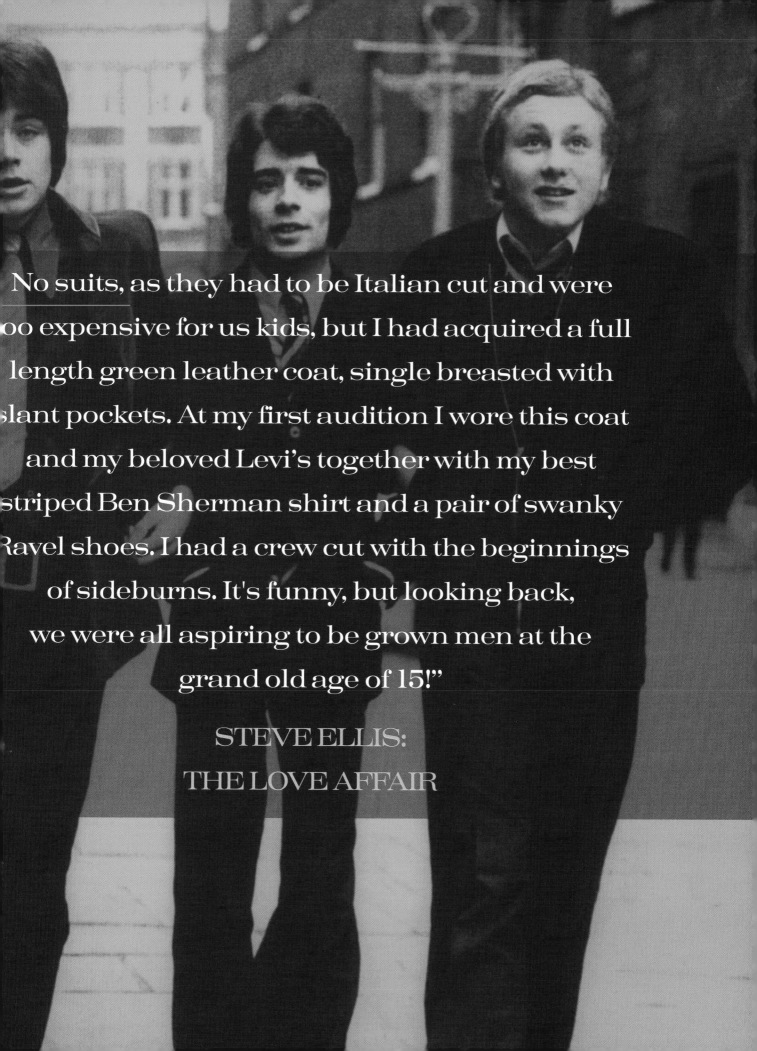

No suits, as they had to be Italian cut and were too expensive for us kids, but I had acquired a full length green leather coat, single breasted with slant pockets. At my first audition I wore this coat and my beloved Levi's together with my best striped Ben Sherman shirt and a pair of swanky Ravel shoes. I had a crew cut with the beginnings of sideburns. It's funny, but looking back, we were all aspiring to be grown men at the grand old age of 15!"

STEVE ELLIS:
THE LOVE AFFAIR

"The factory was about twenty-six feet long," she recalls. "I used to be a machinist. There were the two sisters and then there was Heather who did the button holes and the buttons. There weren't many of us, ten at the most. Jean and Carol were more in charge of different bits. I think Jean was in charge of the machinists and Carol looked after more of the cutting and the dispatch side."

Part of Dorothy's job was to place each shirt in a special box. The original boxes had a brown wood effect with Ben's signature written in black and orange upon them.

"In those days," she recalls, "it was on a board which had two pieces sticking up that you got the collar round. Then you put a bit of plastic round the top collar button and round the shirt to keep it stiff, then you folded the shirt behind the board and put a pin in. In some cases you had a dozen pins. People always used to say that just when you thought you'd got them all out, you'd put on the shirt and there'd be another one!"

Business was good. The shirts not only appealed to men of all ages but were gaining serious favour with the youth cult known as Mods. Yet Ben could not rest on his button-downs just yet. All financial rewards had to be ploughed straight back into the business.

"The orders kept coming in," Daphne Sherman recalls, "but the thing was he didn't have the money to bring the cloth over from America. He didn't want to use the cloth that was here, it had to be the special American Oxford cloth. He had all these orders so he took them to his bank manager and got some money. Then he was able to get Dan River, who were the manufacturers in New York, to ship out the cloth to England. He had to do that quite a few times until he had enough turnover. At the time, his staff were taking wages but he wasn't.'"

Daphne and Ben first crossed each other's paths in 1963 at a popular Brighton coffee bar called Andy's. They didn't speak but they did notice each other. Both were married with children, a one-year-old son named Marcus in Daphne's case.

"I used to see Ben around Brighton," Daphne recalls, "and every time he saw me, he would go, 'Hi Daph.' I used to run a mile. I saw that glint in his eye."

"He was a very handsome fellow," says Jack Lyons, "and he was also a very likeable fellow."

Ben and Daphne were formally introduced at a party thrown by a mutual acquaintance named Barry Langford. As Ben's behaviour that night suggested he was after something a bit more serious than a casual affair, Daphne started taking a bit more interest in this cigar-loving individual who adored the music of Louis Prima.

She realised just how serious he was, when during a chance meeting in the street, Daphne told Ben that she, her husband and child were moving to a new house on Brighton's South Downs. Within a month, Ben had bought a house near to them.

Yet Daphne refused to countenance Ben and remained out of reach to him, literally so, when she and her family left for a long stay in Australia. However, when Daphne returned, it was with her son, not her husband. They had split up. Ben called her as soon as he heard she was home.

"The first thing I said," she recalls, "was 'how are your wife and kids?' He said, 'they've left me and gone back to California.' I didn't believe him. He kept ringing, but I wouldn't go out with him. A year later he rang and told me that he had opened up a showroom on Carnaby Street and to come up and have lunch there. My curiosity got the better of me. I met him at the showroom (opposite the John Stephen shop on the corner of Kingly and Carnaby Street). It was Christmas time and all the fairy lights were on. There was an incredible atmosphere and it felt so great to be back in England in the '60s. The showroom was just magic, seeing all the different coloured shirts. But the thing that struck me was how good Ben looked. He was slim and extremely well dressed. He was in his usual style of sports jacket, button-down shirt and trousers. He also wore Brut - which, believe it or not, was considered trendy then - because at that time he was the sole agent for Faberge."

The Carnaby Street showroom was not the only acquisition the Ben Sherman company had their eye on. They were also interested in a property at 31 Duke Street, Brighton. Ben had decided he wanted to open his own shirt shop and in 1967 that's precisely what he did. Naturally, it had a unique element to its inception.

Philip Labatto was a shirt enthusiast ('a fetishist, really') who since leaving his family home, had spent much of his time abroad. One Saturday morning, during a quick visit to his parents, Philip's father had suggested they take a car ride around Brighton.

"He said to me," Labatto recalls, "'Look at this street, Duke Street, it's just like Carnaby Street used to be. It's off the main road, there are links to the post office, it's near The Lanes and, oh look, there's a shop for lease called Jade House.' I said, 'How interesting,' and never thought anything more about it."

Not long after their journey, there was a knock on the front door. It was Ben Sherman.

"When I opened the door," Labatto says, "'he said in his usual way, 'Hi, I'm Ben Sherman.' I knew the name because I used to buy American shirts. I said, 'You make shirts don't you?' He said, 'Yeah, I do.' He

came in the house, we had a few drinks, next thing I know he says to me, 'I've always wanted to open a shirt shop.' I said, 'How strange, so have I.' So he says, 'Hey, listen, jump in the car and I'll show you a property that I'm looking at.' In those days you could drive down Duke Street and there was the shop, Jade House. I said to Ben, 'Do you know, my father showed me this shop this morning? Isn't that funny?' Next thing I know, we are back at my house and we agree to go into partnership."

DAPHNE AND BEN
MAJORCA, PALMA NOVA, 1966

Two years later, Philip discovered the truth. The whole thing had been a set up! Unbeknownst to him, Sherman had met Philip's father the week before on a train to Brighton. On discovering that he made shirts, Philip's father exclaimed, "I'd love you to meet my son. He's crazy about shirts and has always wanted to open a shirt shop." At which point Ben replied, "Hey, so do I."

Philip's father was keen to keep his son in Brighton hence the plan he hatched with Sherman on the Brighton train. "Ben, as you've probably heard," Labatto says, "was a great salesman. He could sell ice to the Eskimos."

Did the smasher dislike Ho?

Shirts in the window of The Jade House, in Duke Street, Brighton, spelled the word "love," but a vandal last night hurled a stone through the glass and scattered the lot. The manager, Mr. Philip Lobaitte, believes that the stone may have been thrown because a photograph of Ho Chi Minh, the North Vietnamese leader, formed part of the display. He said: "It put it in the window in the letter 'O' of the word love, in support of last week's anti-war demonstration, and perhaps someone objected. Posters on the outside have been defaced before, but no one has ever broken the window."

Jade House opened in 1967. Local historian, Geoff Mead, recalls visiting the shop.

"In those days, gentlemen's clothes shops sold everything from cufflinks to shoes," he recalls. "But this shop just sold shirts and it was amazing. The first shirt I bought in there was bright orange, pure cotton, a lovely kind of shiny finish and it had a white button down collar with white cuffs."

Another customer to the shop was Michael Lowrie, a local salesman.

"It had no counters," he say of Jade House. "It was very laid back. Everyone dressed casually and it was all youngsters who worked there. A lot of people used to go shopping there and the social circle became the same. Everyone was doing the same things so they all knew each other."

Lowrie worked for a popular clothes shop named Gog and he relied upon the Ben Sherman company, above all others, to supply them with quality goods.

"That was the difficulty at the time," Lowrie recalls, "finding manufacturers who weren't making crappy stuff. My background is proper tailoring so I couldn't buy rubbish, it had to be of good quality and Ben Sherman was good quality. It was the Ivy League style, but then he put it into different fabrics and checks and made shirts that were different."

A few months after opening Jade House, Ben and Phil decided a more suitable shop name was required. Ben asked Labatto to think up some ideas and then draw them on paper.

"First one I drew," he remembers, "was a Rolling Stones song, '2000 Light Years From Home.' Then I did 'Millions Of Shirts Inc.' I showed Ben the first one. He said, 'What the fuck does that mean?' I said, 'It's a track on the new Rolling Stones album.'

He said, 'What's the other one?' I said, "Millions of Shirts Inc.' He went, 'That's the one!' Then I got a letter from someone saying you can't use Inc. in England. So we called it Millions Of Shirts Inc. Ltd."

John Upton, a well-known local artist, was hired to paint the outside of the shop. His work adorned many Brighton shop-fronts and walls but probably none was as memorable as his work for Ben and Philip.

"I said to him," Labotto says, "'these are pictures of the shirts, so do something like that.' But what he did was, he painted all these zebras and lions and tigers with his naked wife either riding them or being attacked by them or being sexually assaulted by them! I said, 'No, that won't do! I don't care what happens to the woman but she's got to wear a shirt!' So he had to repaint the scene and in the end the mural looked great."

RARE BEN SHERMAN SHIRTS
FROM THE 60s.

MORE RARE BEN SHERMAN SHIRTS FROM THE 60s AND 70s, EXHIBITED AT THE BRIGHTON & HOVE MUSEUM & ART GALLERY, SUMMER 2003

Despite the unique nature of Millions Of Shirts Inc. Ltd, the shop's turnover did not match the pair's initial financial projections.

"We always had a lot of stock but not the stock that was wanted, the skinhead stock," Bill Knightsbridge reflects. "We used to sell all these things Ben created but we never took that much money."

Undeterred, two more shops followed, both in London. The first was on the Queensway Road. Ben and Daphne lived in nearby Moscow Road and one night on an evening stroll, Ben noticed a small barber's shop. He crossed over, peered into the window. "This would make a great shirt shop", he told Daphne. Soon after, he approached the owner, a Michael Grant who just by co-incidence was tiring of the hair cutting business and was looking for a new business venture.

"No money was exchanged," Daphne recalls. "They took out the barber's stuff and put in fittings for a shirt shop at the front. The barber fittings went to the back of the shop, down a corridor which then opened up into a nice space. Ben then brought in his cousin Elaine, who'd done her training with Michael John, along with her friend Corrine. He had no problem with the bank in setting them up in business, that's how bankable his name was. I was called in to work at both London shops when things got really busy, and the only time Ben would ever appear was when he wanted to raid the tills!"

The Brompton Road shop was situated in Beauchamp Place and as befitted its grand location, specialised in 'custom-made' shirts.

"We used to have people come in and say they were looking for a Ben Sherman shirt. We would say, 'They are all Ben Sherman shirts.' They would say, 'No! I want a Ben

NEW FROM SHERMAN— MILLIONS OF SHIRTS

BEN SHERMAN, the man who made a great name and a lot of money from making shirts, is set to repeat the performance, but from the other side of the business, retailing, writes ROGER KIDD.

Under the banner "Millions of Shirts," he intends to set up a chain of retail outlets across the country. At present he has three shops, but recently he signed a franchise deal with a large public company. [...] open shops-within-shops in its 200 branches.

The first six will begin to trade in September and by Christmas a further 10 will have been added. By the middle of 1974 around 80 should be trading and it is possible he will eventually use the whole 200

"I hope other companies will be interested and like to take a slice of the action," says Mr. Sherman. "The franchisee gets the same return as if he were running the operation himself but he has no aggravation."

BEN SHERMAN
Signed a franchise

FROM TOP: MILLIONS OF SHIRTS MURAL,
BEN IN DRAG FOR FANCY DRESS PROMOTION,
PAM STEPHENSON, BRIGHTON 1968

DAVE DEE, DOZY, BEAKY, MICK AND TICH, 1966
BUT POSSIBLY NOT IN THAT ORDER...
DAVE IS ON THE FAR LEFT AND TICH AT THE TOP

"The band were looking for something different and colourful to perform in, and Tich was wearing this LOVELY Ben Sherman shirt on stage - it looked great. I liked it so much I went out and got one, a button-down, all multicoloured stripes. Then all the band started wearing them, so much so that when we played a gig at the Walthamstow Theatre in East London, nearly all the Mods in the audience had them on."
DAVE DEE
DAVE DEE, DOZY, BEAKY
MICK & TICH

"In the early Sixties, shirts with button-down collars were very different from the norm, and you could still wear one with a tie, or a cravat - it was such a great look I decided to wear my Ben Sherman shirts on stage. That was another thing about Bens - there were so many colours to choose from, they were amazing. My first one was a pale blue button-down in the soft Oxford cloth they did, but I was always into the brighter colours - my favourite bright red one was beautiful - I wore it on stage a lot, and I remember Beaky wore a great pink one. We were the first band to wear Ben Shermans on stage, and now nearly 40 years later my son tells me I still must wear my Ben Sherman shirts on stage. Its all come full circle!"
TICH (IAN AMEY):
DAVE DEE, DOZY, BEAKY
MICK & TICH

THE N'BETWEENS 1966 - JIM LEA, DON POWELL, NODDY HOLDER, DAVE HILL - BEFORE THEY CUT THEIR HAIR AND BECAME PROTO-SKINHEAD BAND AMBROSE SLADE (OPPOSITE PAGE AT BOTTOM) - THEN THEY RE-GREW IT AND BECAME JUST PLAIN OLE 'SLADE'
TOP OPPOSITE - BAD MANNERS' BUSTER BLOODVESSEL - PROOF THAT BEN SHERMAN CAN CATER FOR THE LARGER SKIN

Sherman shirt!' What they meant was they all wanted the classic button-down!"

"I'd never worn button-down shirts" says Geoff Mead, "and I'd certainly never seen this loop on the back or a button. In those days you walked down the street and you saw someone wearing a Ben Sherman shirt, well there was no other shirt like it. Now you can get shirts which look like a Ben Sherman, the right materials, and same type of thing. But in those days, there were no others."

The shirts retailed at two fixed prices. A basic Ben Sherman shirt would set you back two pounds, nineteen shillings and sixpence. A more flamboyant number would come in at three pounds, two shillings and sixpence, which wasn't much of an increase for a one-off customised article. This of course appealed to the more discerning customer, particularly the Mods.

In 1964, those very same shirts were worn by Mods fighting Rockers on Brighton beach. It could only mean one thing; Mod was dead. It had become too popular, too well known. Most of its power had lay in its secrecy but when the *Daily Mirror* knows what you're up to then you are rendered weak.

Disgusted by the public behaviour of those now calling themselves Mods, a new younger breed appeared on the scene. They eschewed casual Mod clothing - parkas, desert boots - and instead opted for a much smarter Ivy League look that recalled the conservative style of the original Mods.

To further distinguish themselves from the masses, this new generation began cutting their hair in a very severe fashion. For three years they would be known by a variety of names (Peanut Head, Baldie) but in September 1969, the *Daily Mirror* referred to them as skinheads and the name has been with us ever since.

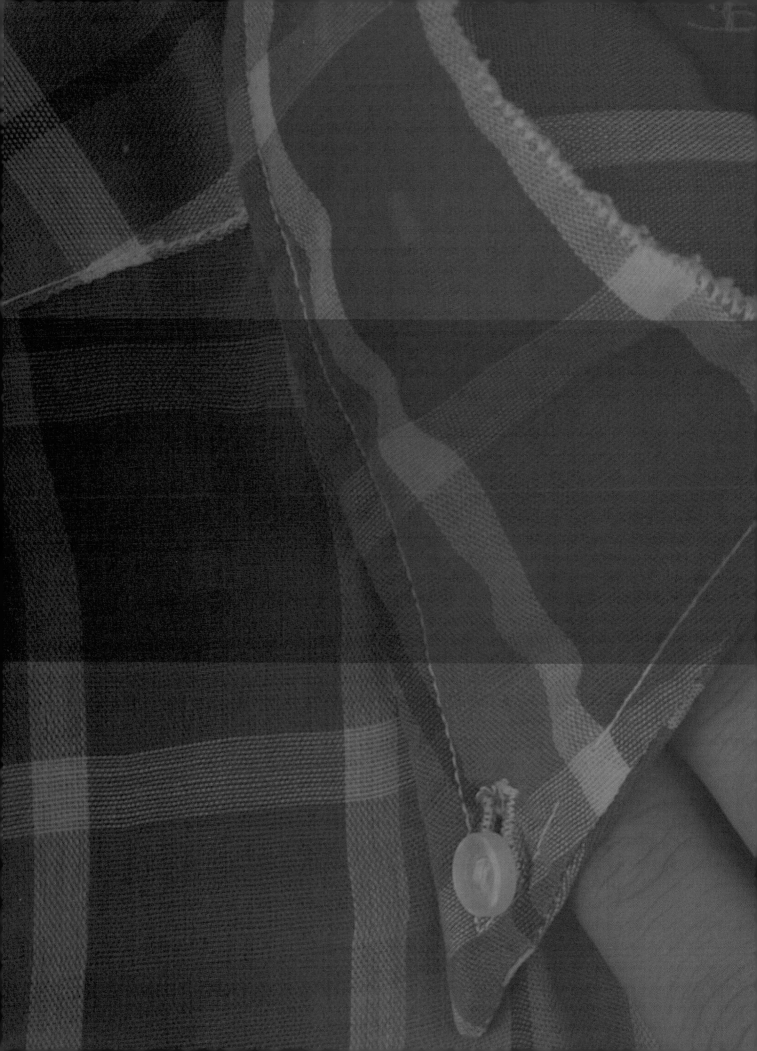

"The original skinhead ones
had about three and a half inch collars.
They were much bigger than the
present day shirts, you could get
three fingers in the collars!"

JOHN BYRNE:
BRIGHTON SKINHEAD 1970

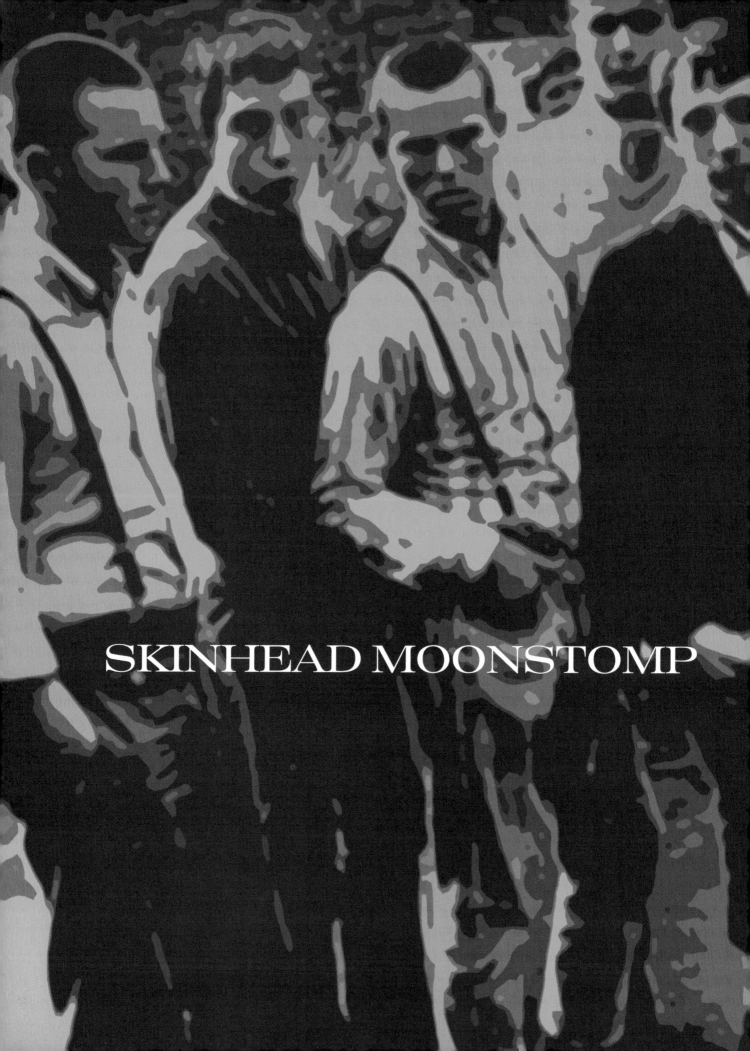

The Mods' durable army parka was replaced by a weighty, council-issue donkey jacket, and desert boots and loafers were replaced by heavy-duty work boots like Doc Martens or monkey boots. There was also a spell of skinheads wearing a steel toe capped variety polished like mirrors, but these were eventually classed as offensive weapons and banned at football matches...unfortunately not before the skinheads endured the weekly humiliation of having their shoelaces confiscated.

Ben Sherman was the shirt of choice. Oxford woven cloth in white and pastel colours followed by stripes and then checks. The Levi's remained, but they were almost entirely dark denim or of an industrial quality held aloft by bright coloured braces that more often than not matched their socks.

Another source of skinhead inspiration and style came from the hip West Indian sections of inner London areas like Lewisham, Notting Hill, and Brixton. The black youths of these areas called themselves 'rude boys' or 'rudies' and were easily identified milling around in their trade mark uniform of long black overcoats called Crombie's, black trousers worn short to reveal white or red

socks, loafers and pork pie hats. By day the accepted image of the skinhead was all boots and braces, but by night that all changed and their dress sense became almost Mod-like. They liked well-tailored suits in petrol blue, shark skin and green and red two tone. Few could afford to have them made but luckily a decent number could be picked up off the peg at places like Burtons or from retailers like Dormeuil. Expensive accessories customised the look, things like cuff links, tie-pins, signet rings and silk handkerchiefs, neatly folded into the top pocket of their Crombie.

As with all teenage cults, hair and haircuts are probably the most important indication as to your particular persuasion. In almost every case it's without doubt the wearer's crowning glory, the finishing touch so to speak. If you go bald prematurely you can't join the gang.

A bald Mod or Ted just doesn't fit the pattern, the haircuts are simply too distinctive. All hair is crucial, always has been, whether it was the slicked back barnet and pencil moustache combination of the post war spivs,

'BENNIED-UP' SKINS AT THE PRINCE BUSTER BENEFIT CONCERT FOR FELLOW SKA LEGEND LAUREL AITKEN - HELD AT CLUB SKA, JANUARY 2004
PHOTOGRAPHER: ANDY GILLARD

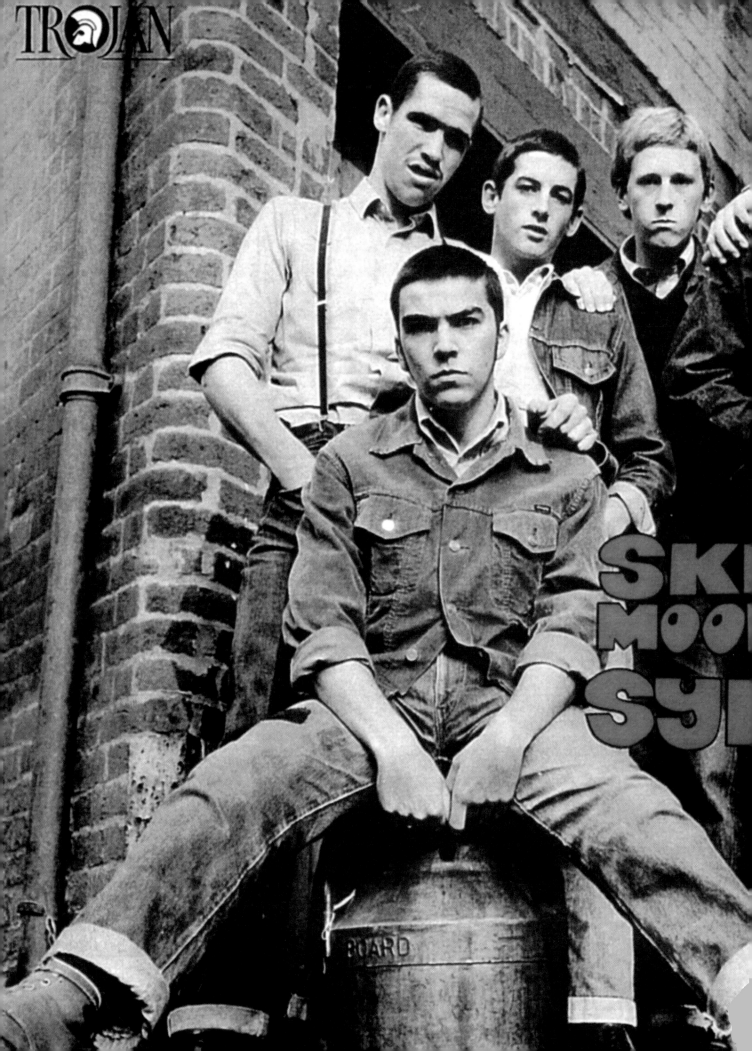

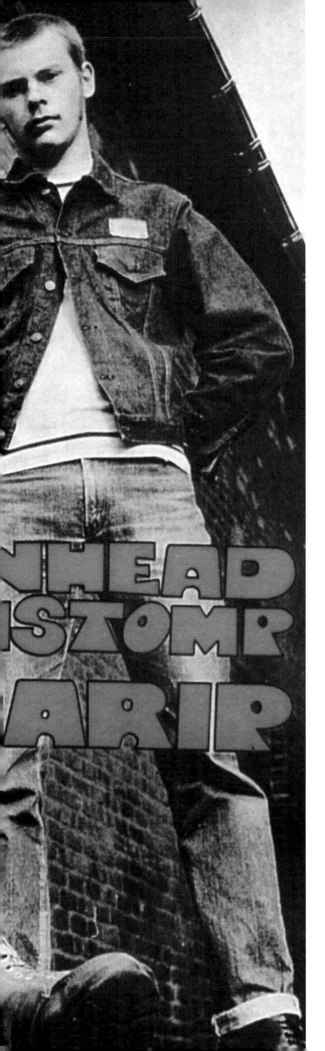

or be-goateed trad jazzers' facial fuzz, they all made a point. Although the trad jazzer did favour a little black beret.

Skinheads would seem to be the exception to this rule, but even they started out with a few hirsute variations before almost unanimously settling on the completely bald look or what they called the 'dark shadow'.

The harder Mods that eventually evolved into the skinheads had already sported cropped hair as early as 1964, as evidenced in the seaside riots that year, but the term 'skinhead' was only ever used by US servicemen stationed in the UK. Then the hairstyle was known as a crew cut - a very close cut with a razored back and sides.

The actual skinhead cut was originally achieved using the plastic safety guard that clipped onto the barbers electric razor. These guards had four thicknesses to them, ranging from the shortest, number one, up to number four. Partings were shaved into the crop from front to crown, which was another idea pinched from the West Indians who'd been parting their hair like that for years.

Moustaches and beards were definitely a no-go but some skins took to growing incredibly long sideburns, nicknamed muttonchops. By 1969 some skinheads, tired of constantly maintaining their crop, decided to grow them out. This gave rise to a whole new group called the 'suedeheads'. These suedeheads had hair at least one to one and a half inches long, which was neatly combed and parted to the side. This trend continued and progressed until the hair reached collar length and these one-time skins renamed themselves the 'smoothies'.

These cults, although not as popular as in their heyday of the late 60s and early 80s revival, continue to flourish in small pockets throughout the world.

"I'm the proud owner of many Bens, but my first recollection of getting a Ben was in the late 60s. I must have been nine or ten. I remember pestering my mum for ages to get me this shirt that I'd seen in the local menswear shop. As soon as I got home with it I put it on and spent the next hour

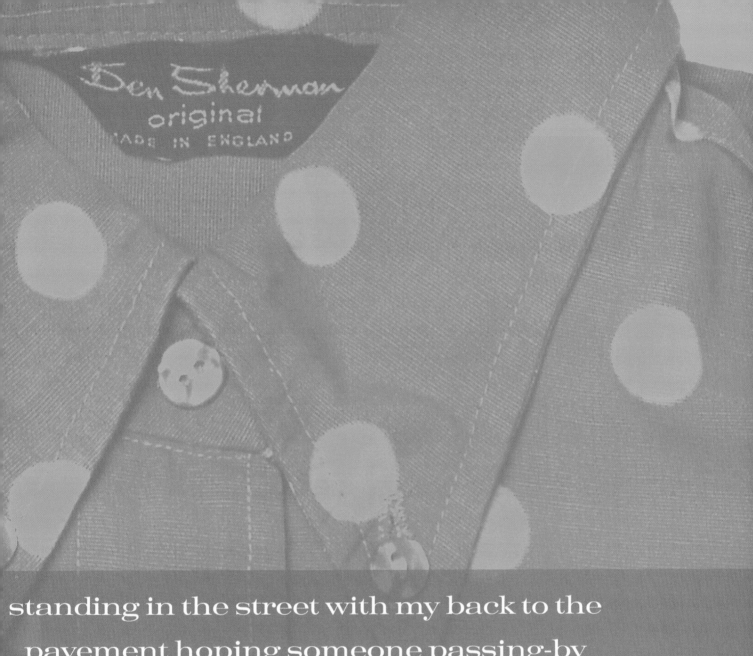

standing in the street with my back to the
pavement hoping someone passing-by
would notice the details, the back collar
button, pleat and hook. Nobody went by.
Didn't matter though...
I knew it looked good."

MARTIN MASON: THE CHORDS

ONLY FABULOUS

THE SMALL FACES - MAKING FULL USE OF THEIR LORD JOHN ACCOUNT FACILITY, 1966

Ben Sherman was a good employer, many say. Sensitive to his workforce, generous too.

"Oh yeah, Ben was a good boss," Dorothy Cole confirms. "We had a laugh with him. I remember he took us out on an outing to the Isle of Wight. I lost my camera and he bought me a new one."

Bill Knightsbridge: "We used to go out on outings and it was unbelievable. I mean one year we went to Paris. None of us had been abroad before, never ever, so it was mind-boggling. That's the kind of employer I remember him as. He was very much a model employer."

If Sherman had an Achilles heel it was his quick fire temper. Yet Ronnie Wiseman strenuously claims he never lost it within the working environment.

"That was outside of business," Wiseman firmly states. "I saw him lose his temper a few times. I've been in restaurants where he lost it because they didn't have what he wanted on the menu. I've been on planes where we were nearly thrown off because the stewards wouldn't give him the seat he wanted. Then again I've been at parties that are dead and Ben would walk in and within half an hour the place was swinging. But you must remember one thing - he was a character and no character is perfect otherwise they are not a character."

1968 would prove to be a notable year for Ben Sherman, both personally and in business. That was the year he married Daphne, launched his first collection for women - "All he did was elongate the shirt into a mini dress with a belt," says Daphne - and moved production, first to Gloucester, then to Northern Ireland. There were two compelling reasons to move. The first was that Ben had made a deal with a company called Trubanised who specialised in

BEN SHERMAN SHIRT DRESSES

separate shirt collars. Unfortunately, the demand for their items had dwindled and they now owned several empty factories. One of them was in Gloucester and another in Londonderry, Northern Ireland.

At the same time, Ronnie Wiseman had spotted an advert in *Menswear* magazine for a firm in Gloucester who specialised in what was termed 'CMT' – Cut Make and Trim. The deal was simple. You supplied the company with the fabrics and the designs, and they produced them for you.

It made sense for Ben Sherman to open up a factory nearby and to start off loading some of their work to the CMT people. The workforce needed all the help they could get. Orders for shirts were now outstripping every other Ben Sherman product, achieving order numbers that the company would soon be unable to meet.

Thousands upon thousands of young working class kids were feverishly buying these essential clothing items and in the process they made Ben Sherman a fortune. This huge demand for the button-down shirt was mainly emanating from the skinhead community. As already discussed, the look was comprised of Levi's jeans, braces, Harrington jackets, Dr Marten shoes and a Ben Sherman shirt.

Part of Ben's fortune could also be located in the explosion of interest in football that followed England's 1966 World Cup win. By the early 70s the improved infrastructure of Great Britain allowed football fans to travel easily for the first time across the country in support of their team. Football violence now became commonplace and many skinheads needed utility clothing. Hence the move away from the smart Ivy League look to the uniform described above. By following their team around England, the London skinheads spread their unique street fashion to all the major cities.

tendre

NUMERO
204
5 pages
SPECIAL

A-CHER: 24 PAGES DE COIFFURES

QUILLAGE DE TWIGGY CLO

T'AMOUR 2 JEUX ELECTIO

68 SHEILA ALAIN DELON ETC

JULES RIMET CUP

WORLD CHAMPIONSHIP JULY 11th - 30th 1966

A measure of Ben Sherman's massive popularity at this juncture can be gauged by the order the Ben Sherman company placed in 1970 with the cloth supplier, Dan River in New York. It requested a million yards of Oxford cloth and a quarter of a million of Gingham material. And just for good measure, the company also bought a quarter of a million yards of colourful striped material.

That year, orders for Ben Sherman shirts rose to 42,000 a week. Unfortunately, the company could only produce 35,000. Their competitors in the market were quick to react. Brutus and Jaytex shirts began manufacturing similar styled shirts (checked button-downs) and were soon viewed as major rivals to the Sherman shirt. Even Ben Sherman employee Bill Knightsbridge found it impossible to resist.

"Somewhere in that period, 1970, 1971," remembers Bill, "there were people on the phone to me every single day of the week saying, 'Why don't you do this? Why don't you do that?' in terms of a fashion shirt. But Ben wasn't into that sort of manufacturing. It was all men's shirts in bright colours with these enormous collars. I took advantage and left and began manufacturing my own shirts. It made no difference to Ben Sherman Ltd. They were sold out twelve months of the year anyway."

Ironically, another person who fell victim to Ben Sherman's huge success was Sherman himself. As demand spectacularly soared, the company was forced to concentrate more and more on shirt production. Ben, who saw himself as a designer first, kept coming up with ideas for new ranges but the demand for his shirts surpassed their importance.

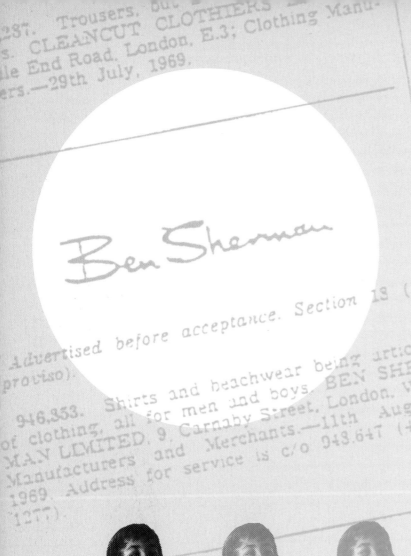

"He carried on designing these great collections which were very well received," Knightsbridge recalls, "but a lot of it wasn't practical to manufacture. The real demand was for the button-down Oxford shirts and the factory couldn't make enough of them. Interestingly enough, he continued putting together collections. I'd see him in New York because he used to attend British fashion week there and he'd have his collections with him. They were very exotic and imaginative but they never sold or got delivered because the factories were too busy making the skinhead merchandise."

Following Ben and Daphne's wedding reception at the Café Royal, Piccadilly, Ben travelled to Cologne for the 1968 German menswear exhibition. The results of their hard work was now becoming tangible. Up until then Sherman was driving a brown Ford. That became a white Jaguar which in turn became a white Rolls Royce. Holidays in Tenerife, the Bahamas, ('a trip to open up bank accounts,' Daphne states) and South Africa proved the good life had arrived. It was all theirs.

"When it was a small business he could cope," Wiseman says. "When it became a big business it wasn't that he couldn't cope, it was that he didn't want to cope. He employed people to do the job. He would turn up at the office, sometimes at eleven in the morning, sometimes at twelve."

By now Ronnie was spending a lot of his time at the Londonderry factory in Northern Ireland. The British government at the time had introduced highly attractive tax breaks in the hope it would entice new business to the province. They also hoped that a booming economy would help assuage the 'troubles' tearing the place apart. The Ben Sherman company had taken full advantage of this incentive and was fast becoming the biggest employer of women in the country.

Despite the terrible violence around them, the Ben Sherman factory was never bombed or harmed. Both Catholics and Protestants loved and wore the shirt. No way would they harm its production. Some things, sometimes, really are beyond prejudice.

In 1970, Sherman made a master move. He introduced a children's range of Ben Sherman clothes. As Daphne Sherman explains, "Ben decided to make Ben Sherman shirts in boyswear and all those little boys have grown up now. So what's the first shirt they are going to buy? The Ben Sherman, of course."

Daphne's ten-year old son, Marcus, wore the first prototype of the shirt in a rare Ben Sherman advert. The company wasn't big on advertising. After all, why waste money when your product is subject to the best advertising of all, namely word of mouth?

In December 1972, the Ben Sherman company newsletter carried a startling front-page item. Ben Sherman had sold the company to the Northern Ireland Finance Corporation. "This is a great day for the company," Ben told his workforce, "a day when I can see its future assured. We are already one of the largest clothing manufacturers in Northern Ireland, and one of the three largest shirt houses in the UK and Ireland. We are determined to become the market leader, and with this new financial structure our objectives can now be achieved much sooner. Any company, which has grown as rapidly as ours - twelve fold in four years - must suffer inevitable growing pains and new finance will help reduce this. But of greater concern to us is the future of the people who work with us, be they our youngest cutter in Kennedy or our salesman in Cologne. The new finance is being used to back the strength and stability of our proven workforce in the factories throughout Ireland.

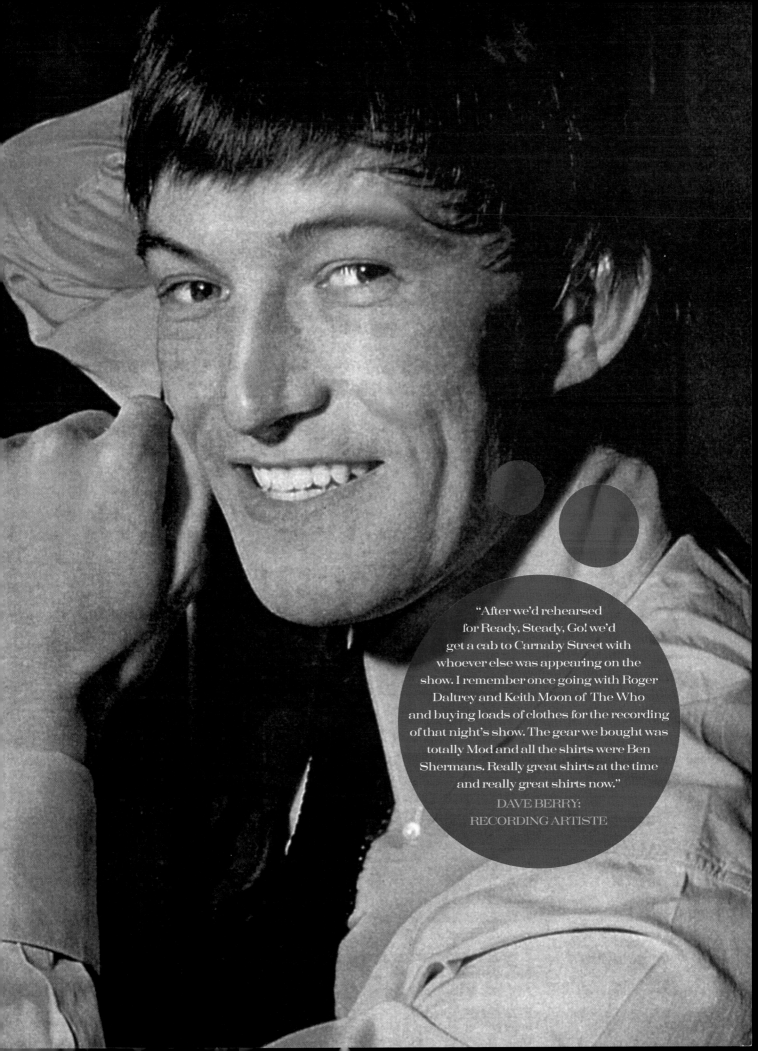

"After we'd rehearsed for Ready, Steady, Go! we'd get a cab to Carnaby Street with whoever else was appearing on the show. I remember once going with Roger Daltrey and Keith Moon of The Who and buying loads of clothes for the recording of that night's show. The gear we bought was totally Mod and all the shirts were Ben Shermans. Really great shirts at the time and really great shirts now."

DAVE BERRY:
RECORDING ARTISTE

I am very confident about the future and feel certain that all of us can look forward to increasing prosperity, with the help of the financial backing and advice we have received." Sherman remained a major part of the company but the writing was on the wall.

"The problem was that Ben lost control," Daphne says, "his finger wasn't on the pulse. They retained him as a designer and a figurehead but he lost control and that didn't suit his personality. It was a clash of the titans and Ben finally walked away from it."

In 1973, Sherman sold his shares and rights and with Daphne in tow headed out to Australia. His plan was to start a new Ben Sherman company. Their trip took five weeks. When the pair arrived and went to trade mark the name Ben Sherman they discovered they had been beaten to the punch. By the company he had just sold.

Sherman tried other business ventures in Australia, some good, some bad. Meanwhile, he and Daphne split up and in 1987, at the age of 62, Ben was taken into hospital for a heart bypass operation.

"The trouble was," says Jack Lyons "all the family had heart trouble and they didn't do anything about it. Ben said he would try and lose weight when he went to Australia. I think he did try but it didn't do any good. All the family - my wife and the sisters and the brothers - they all died of heart trouble."

Six weeks after his operation, Ben fell into an argument with the porter in his block of flats and his heart gave way for good. He was just 62.

"He was an enigma," Daphne says of her late husband. "I remember when people used to say to him 'what is the secret of your success?' and he would sit there and smile and say, 'I got lucky.' But you see, in the beginning the amount of work he put in, the mental aggravation he went through because of the negativity he got, he still carried on and he did so because he knew what he wanted. Persistent, he was persistent."

Ronnie Wiseman, who had left the company prior to Sherman but maintained contact, was knocked sideways by his friend's death.

"It was quite a shock," he recalls. "That said, I do not regret one minute of my association with Ben Sherman. I was lucky to know him."

Ben Sherman was a truly unique man, a businessman with an artist's soul. He was restless, energetic and very smart. His contribution to British fashion lasts to this day and his impact on others, most notably his family, is still evident.

Martin Sherman: "He wouldn't tell me how to dress but he would tell me to make sure that I looked good. He wouldn't tell me how to wear my hair, just ensure that I looked good. Same with my room and my belongings, make sure my stuff was good. At a restaurant he would always have me order something good. Quite often, we would eat Indian food, which was unheard of for an American kid back then. Once when I baulked at tasting something, he said this – "How do you know that this won't be the most favourite food in your whole life and you missed it because you were too scared to take a little nibble?" That has turned into my whole life's philosophy. Because of my father I feel obligated to take a little nibble of everything that life gives me."

That last sentence is maybe the finest epitaph we can give Ben Sherman. Or instead, maybe we should turn to the man's trademark phrase. Ronnie Wiseman recalls that when people asked Ben how he was doing, he would always say the same thing…

"Only fabulous," would be the reply.
"Only fabulous."

THE TREMELOES 1967 - ALAN BLAKELY, RICK WEST, DAVE MUNDEN, CHIP HAWKES

"I got my first one when we were booked to play at a posh do. Our record company CBS had taken us all shopping and kitted us out in Ben Sherman. They were fabulous - all the colours of the rainbow. My Mum used to say that she didn't like the 'flower-power' image with the colourful clothes and the beads - she used to say 'for goodness sake, go put on a shirt.' Of course, when it was a Ben Sherman, you didn't mind! They changed the whole fashion perception of shirts, made it a 'young' thing."

LEN (CHIP) HAWKES
THE TREMELOES

"The button-down shirt -
oh yes - we were very aware of that
fashion. The Troggs always wanted to
stand out and wear something eyecatching,
and someone came up with the idea of the candy
striped suits. They weren't something I would have
worn in the street, but they certainly got you noticed.
The trouble was, you couldn't wear shirts with them,
because they were too loud, so we wore black T shirts
underneath. Then when the colourful Ben Sherman
came in, we ditched the suits and wore the shirts with
the coloured stripes. We used to do this thing called
'running the gauntlet' where we ran through the
crowd to the stage. I remember several times,
all I had left by the time I got on stage was
the button-down collar and the cuffs!"

REG PRESLEY:
THE TROGGS

THE TROGGS 1967 - RONNIE BOND, REG PRESLEY, CHRIS BRITTON, PETE STAPLES

"It was the details on the Ben Sherman shirts that were great. Not only did you have button-down collars - I'd never worn a button-down collar till then - but there was even a little button in the middle of the collar at the back... and then below that, and I never knew what it was for,

I never met anyone else who knew what it was for either, but there was a loop - this little loop of material and whether you were supposed to hang it on a hanger I don't know... but it was always there."

MICK WOODHEAD: BRIGHTON MOD 1960s

REVIVAL

"I used to visit Brick Lane second hand market through 1977-79 to hunt down and buy my Bens. I had some great ones, including several slim-fits with the pleat sewn in all the way down the back. Incidentally, there was also a great little shop in Brick Lane that sold old-stock Bens in their original boxes. At the height of the '79 Mod revival I had at one time over 100 fantastic button-downs, nearly all Bens and nearly all of which cost no more than a quid each."

JEFF SHADBOLT: PURPLE HEARTS

THE JAM, 1977
FROM LEFT: BRUCE FOXTON, PAUL 'MODFATHER' WELLER, RICK BUCKLER

"The Jam always wore button-down shirts. Ben Shermans, whatever. I was very influenced by my older brother who was an original Mod. I simply liked the look, and still do".

BRUCE FOXTON: THE JAM

It's not surprising that there was a Mod and Ska revival in England at the end of the 70s, as that particular period of our cultural history will almost certainly never be remembered as a golden age for British fashion.

Punk rock might well have given the British music industry a much needed kick in its loon pants in 1976 and '77 but, let's face it, the Punk look did bugger all to smarten up the nation's youth.

Mind you, if you were an average kid on the street back then and you didn't fancy sticking a safety pin through your nose there really wasn't much of an alternative. The whole of the UK was awash in drip dry shirts, dirty denim and cheesecloth.

That was your choice - there was virtually nothing in between (give or take one or two brief Teddy Boy / Rockabilly revivals, but once again they fizzled out as mysteriously as the originals did). So if you weren't interested in pogoing and spitting on anyone chances are you were either an Afghan coat wearing hippie or you were walking around looking like one of the Fenn Street Gang.

Little wonder then that stylish movements like the Ska and Mod revivals were quickly seized upon and spread like wildfire. However, getting the look right was a taller order than you would have thought.

There were simply no decent clothes in the shops. Straight trousers and jeans didn't exist and the humble button-down was now as rare as last year's snow. So much so, that to own such a thing in those days meant sewing buttons onto collars yourself. This almost got you the required look from a distance, but with the absence of button holes this practice rendered the shirt 'unironable'.

In fact all shirts at this particular time had reached an unprecedented all time low in both shape and style. Collars were

PAUL WELLER IN ACTION AND AGAIN, BELOW, WITH TERRY RAWLINGS AT THE WELLINGTON, WATERLOO, 1979, RECRUITING THE CHORDS AS SUPPORT FOR THE JAM'S DEBUT RAINBOW SHOW

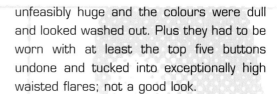

Ben Sherman

original mod
51 Maddox st, London. W.1. 499 8544

SHIRTS IN THE
SHOPS NOW!

Ben Sherman
Original

Ben Sherman Ltd. 51 Maddox St London W1 Tel: 01-499 8544

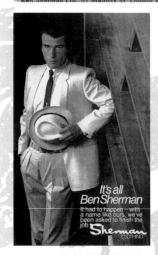

It's all
Ben Sherman

It had to happen - with
a name like ours, we've
been asked to finish the
job
Sherman
CLOTHING

Ben Sherman

unfeasibly huge and the colours were dull and looked washed out. Plus they had to be worn with at least the top five buttons undone and tucked into exceptionally high waisted flares; not a good look.

All-over prints were hugely popular, especially those featuring Marilyn Monroe and any type of 30s gangster imagery. Hawaiian scenes were also big sellers and any print that showed early modes of transport, like the penny farthing or tri-winged aircraft simply flew off the shelves. Shoes were still of the stack heeled variety and kipper ties were expanding at a terrifying rate.

Things were so bad that in order to unearth any authentic 60s style items or period American styles you were forced to rummage for hours on end through musty, dusty boxes of clobber either in second-hand thrift shops, jumble sales or old men's retailers.

Bizarre then that movements that prided themselves on looking neat, sharp, smart and clean initially relied on clothing that had probably been donated to charity shops by the relatives of dead people.

Still, this didn't stop the determined. They adapted their wardrobes and doggedly tracked down the odd gem of a jacket or a spot on pair of shoes in the back streets of South London and the East End. It was a slow process but then in the summer of 1979 The Who released their film version of the album *Quadrophenia* and the whole scene exploded... cool clothes were suddenly available, including a new range of hitherto unobtainable Ben Sherman shirts, Lambrettas were back on the roads and the beaches were once again full of Bank Holiday 'bovver'.

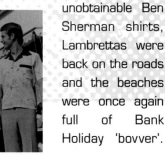

14 April 1979   US $1.50c/Canada 80c   20p

NEW MUSICAL EXPRESS

NME

MODS
Bank Holiday Battles Revisited

Scooters
Clothes
Riots
Rhythm
& Blues
MOD MEMORIES
pages 28-31

SECRET AFFAIR, *SMASH HITS* COVER, 1979
C/W FROM TOP: DENNIS SMITH, DAVE CAIRNS, IAN PAGE, SEB SHELTON

SMASH HITS

FORTNIGHTLY

September 20-October 3 1979 **25p**

SECRET AFFAIR

Words to the TOP SINGLES including

Cruel To Be Kind

Don't Bring Me Down

Love's Gotta Hold On Me

The who

COMMODORES

**JAM
JOE JACKSON
in colour**

Message In A Bottle

By The Police On A&M

Just a castaway an island lost at sea — O
Anuzzer lonely day no-one here but me — O
More loneliness than any man could bear
Rescue me before I fall into despair — O

(All the words inside)

By then Punk Rock had all but blown over. The Sex Pistols were gone, The Clash 'selling out' in America, The Buzzcocks were faltering and surviving bands like The Vibrators, The Lurkers and Slaughter & The Dogs... well no one really cared about them in the first place.

The cinematic story of a Mod called Jimmy Cooper searching for his identity while getting pilled out of his socks and enjoying beach brawls and alfresco sex hit the right note.

Having emerged at the height of Punk in 1977, The Jam ultimately won out and became one of the biggest British bands of all time. They also led the charge for a whole glut of younger mod outfits shadowing the band, that by 1980 included groups like The Chords, The Purple Hearts, and Secret Affair - some of whom had been vying for recognition for well over a year or more and all of whom went on to achieve some chart success and inspire new generations of similarly influenced bands from The Stone Roses and The Charlatans to Ocean Colour Scene and Oasis.

That 1979 revival was the rebirth of a movement and an image that has remained visible ever since. Its many elements are firmly ingrained in our society and, like the Ben Sherman button-down, recognised the world over as something typically English.

THE CREAM OF THE '79 MOD REVIVAL. BELOW L-R:
SECRET AFFAIR, LONG TALL SHORTY, MERTON PARKAS (BELOW),
THE CHORDS, PURPLE HEARTS, THE LAMBRETTAS (BELOW)

...fine French brandy
can afford to share with friends

"In the Groovies,
we took our look very
seriously, and we didn't feel
well dressed without a nice suit and a
decent shirt. It made us feel very
secure in our own smug way.
In the end I had a whole wardrobe
full of gorgeous Ben Shermans..."

CHRIS WILSON:
THE FLAMIN' GROOVIES

"Almost everybody I knew in 1980 who 'became a Mod' couldnt afford to buy a Ben Sherman. The obligatory uniform in those days was Clarks Hush Puppies, a pair of sta press and a blue or black Brutus Trim Fit shirt from Milletts in Kingston. Bennies were for the bigger boys and rich kids. 18 months later and I was treated to my very first brand new Ben Sherman. Blue with white stripes (or white with blue stripes depending on your view of life) £10.99 from Carnaby Street. Fitted like a glove, with a collar that never frayed no matter how much you moved your neck from side to side. Then disaster struck. Somebody had an accident at work and bled all over the carpet tiles in the bosses' office. Without me knowing they changed the bourgeois tiles for the ones in MY dark room! The dark room wasn't just my place of work, it was also a place of rest and most dinner hours were spent having a kip to compensate for the hectic life style of an 18 year old Mod. I retired for my daily snooze and awoke an hour later to find my back drenched and my blue Ben Sherman stained crimson. Gutted, I took my issues up with management and cleverly knocked up a receipt for £20 (being a typesetter had its advantages). The money went straight on my next two shirts and became the start of a long and happy relationship between myself and Mr Sherman. Incidentally, my Mum washed the stained shirt twice and all the blood had come out. Quality, see? Shirt brands come and go but 25 years on, we are still in love."

PAUL HALLAM: CLUB DJ AND EX-DARKROOM MONKEY

"All of The Specials, when not wearing polo shirts, wore Ben Shermans on stage, and off! We would look for bargains in second-hand shops in Coventry. Sometimes we'd get lucky and find Ben Sherman shirts in nearly new condition. As we became more famous we could afford to buy four or five Bennies at a time. Extravagant?"

RODDY BYRES:
THE SPECIALS

"A little gang of us discovered
a tiny old fashioned tailors tucked
away in The Cut at Waterloo. It was an
absolute gold mine... I remember they just
had boxes & boxes of Mod style clothes with
racks of sta press and, to our delight, loads of old
Bennies. Trying to keep that place secret was a
nightmare! Funny, looking back now, I reckon that
doing all that was part of the fun of being a Mod.
All the searching around for classic button-
downs. I guess we thought we were
being different. Stylish. Anyway, best not
to analyse it too much. Just happy days."
BILLY HASSETT:
THE CHORDS

"Nine Below Zero wore
nothing but Ben Shermans
for the first few years on the road.
They looked good on stage no matter
how hot and sweaty you got. We'd mainly
go for white or black, like the old Blues
guys wore, but they were a bastard
to find in the late 70's - different story
now though - thankfully. "

DENNIS GREAVES:
NINE BELOW ZERO

THE UNDERTONES, 1979
L-R: DAMIAN O'NEILL, FEARGAL SHARKEY, JOHN O'NEILL, MICKEY BRADLEY, BILLY DOHERTY - GOD BLESS 'EM

"It wasn't until I was 19 when The Undertones were blasting their way through the hit parade that I bought my first Ben Sherman shirt. This was something that you aspired to. I couldn't afford such high fashion gear until then. I loved the shirts, even wearing them on Top Of The Pops. I even wore a Ben Sherman shirt on my wedding day! A body hugging white button-down, very nice. All throughout the career of The Undertones I have always worn the brand and still do. If Ben Sherman keep making them, then I'm still wearing them."

BILLY DOHERTY :
THE UNDERTONES

"I don't know if this was just
a Northern thing, but people up in
Manchester would always get new clothes
for Whit Sunday and I'd seen a kid wearing
a really cool striped Ben Sherman riding a
Lambretta TV175 scooter. So, a Ben Sherman
was what I really wanted, and that Whitsun I did
finally get my first one. It was a lovely gold and
fawn number and I wore it time and again with a
great pair of black and white checked Small
Faces style hipster trousers from C&A!
Fucking Kink-tastic man!"

STEVE DIGGLE:
THE BUZZCOCKS

THE BUZZCOCKS - AT ODDS WITH THE WORLD, 1980
L-R: JOHN MAHER, STEVE DIGGLE, STEVE GARVEY, PETE SHELLEY

"As a pupil at The Quinton Kynaston School in Camden I was more than delighted when school uniforms were the required necessity. At the age of 13 my Aunt bought me my first Ben Sherman shirt and I wore it to school. It was of course a button-down, in a green pattern check - with the original black & orange label. We gave up our school uniforms and instead we were all running around wearing Ben Sherman shirts. I was very much in fashion that year, and if I say so myself, looked very cool. I still wear Bennies today. They really have passed the test of time though - a great British label. Absolutely."
SUGGS: MADNESS

"I used to go roller skating at Alexandra Palace, and the fashion seemed to be Bens and white Levi's. I was 14, it was the summer and I had on my first Ben Sherman shirt. I suppose I felt pretty cool and proud - important to me in those days... I had to save up for it though, so for me it wasn't like these days where trendy items seem to be so easily attained. I bought it from a shop called Selwyn's in Kentish Town. It was a button-down, with short sleeves, in a lovely multi-colour check pattern - white, orange, blue & yellow. I'm happy that Ben Shermans are still around today - just goes to show that quality always reigns."
CARL (CHAS SMASH) SMYTH: MADNESS - NOT PICTURED

"At the age of 16 I was a skinhead, I followed the pack and followed the style that came with it. The suit, the brogues, the white socks and the Benny. Very slim and very sexy. One day with a bunch of Charlton fans we marched on London, up West to see them play, against who I can't remember. En route we stopped off for some fun in Carnaby Street. On the way home after the game, I presume we lost, we headed back the same way, terrifying locals and tourists as we went. I was one of the crowd, the blob, there at the back running and shouting, being 16 and very stupid. Suddenly a window went in, a shop lay open, in the riot I grabbed what I could, three Ben Sherman shirts. Back home I sneaked them into my room under my parents noses. I had the biggest trophy of the day, three lovely new shirts. Check, smart, thin, sexy. For a young lad quite a catch. These days I have put down the brick for the credit card, it seems to work better for me. The girls always liked the shirt on your back, the pleat and the button-down, I still wear it today, but the girls have become older and so have their attitudes towards men such as me, still boys at heart. Still members of the style council."

COOL BRITANNIA

NOEL GALLAGHER, OASIS. PHOTOGRAPHY: ROGER SARGENT

And then came the 90s, and for a short but glorious period of time the UK looked as though it would once again rule the rock and roll roost. 'Britpop' and 'Cool Britannia' were the new buzzwords and the Union Jack was once again a flag to be proud of.

Oasis and Blur were the new Beatles and Kinks, Primal Scream the Rolling Stones and Pulp's Jarvis Cocker was a new pre-Starman Bowie.

Of course, none of it was new, but then again nor was Ben Sherman. Yet somehow, it all made strange sense. The future of Ben Sherman lay in its past and a new generation was ready to pick up from where it had left off. Britpop undoubtedly breathed new life into a great British brand that like the homegrown music scene had inexplicably lost its way. As a musical movement it shook a drab British fashion industry by the shirt collar and totally revitalized Ben Sherman's image.

DAMAN ALBARN, BLUR FRONTMAN, WEARING HIS COLOURS ON HIS CHEST.
SELECTION OF ADVERTS FROM THE HEIGHT OF THE 90s

"I first came across
Ben Sherman in the
late 60s. I was impressed
with the style and quality
of the shirts - so much so that I had
them in my boutiques in Manchester.
They represent what to my mind
is the best of British.
Funny that coming from
an Irishman!"
GEORGE BEST:
FOOTBALL LEGEND

"It's only fitting that we
should represent 'El Beatle',
football legend George Best.
A true style icon who knows more
than a thing or two about fashion.
Forget David Beckham, George
was the very first sports fashion superstar.
He had his own personalised clothing and
footwear collections, opened his own chain
of boutiques and sold over a million pairs
of George Best Stylo trainers and football
boots in the 70s. A true style pioneer,
on AND off the pitch."
ANDY RIGG:
MARKETING DIRECTOR
BEN SHERMAN

40 YEARS AND ON

Since Ben's untimely demise, the company has changed hands many times. During this period it has tended to concentrate its efforts on the creation and manufacturing of its famous shirts. Since the turn of the new millennium that route has now changed. Knowing that in today's highly competitive market to stagnate is to die, the Ben Sherman company has expanded into fresh new areas.

So where is Ben Sherman now? Well, it's proud to announce that once again it's back at the top of its game - the label has gone full circle and reclaimed its rightful place to become an international British lifestyle brand that has crossed oceans as well as cultures. Ben Sherman is now a massive influence in the global music, entertainment and fashion arenas and can be seen on today's biggest movers and shakers, as it has been for the last four decades... and the best is yet to come.

BEN SHERMAN - ONLY FABULOUS

"Ben Sherman -
a real brand for
real people!"
RIO FERDINAND:
FOOTBALLER

Legends do not come much bigger than George Best. A Northern Ireland lad, Best joined Manchester United at 16 years of age and over the next 10 years stunned the world. The first footballer to be featured on both the front and back page of the *Daily Mirror*, the player whose outrageous skill, verve and style left opponents flummoxed and crowds gasping, the skinny genius of the Manchester United team that conquered Europe, Best's supreme genius changed football forever. Cheeky, young, good looking, Best was a natural magnet for women, the envy of every man. Naturally, he was also a great dresser. Mod Casual in the time of his heyday, suited and booted for the '70s. Appropriately, Best owned three clothes shops in Manchester.

He cared deeply about his appearance so it was no surprise that the Ben Sherman company should work with George on a range of clothing designed for today's market. Both are legendary names in British culture and although Best might have stopped playing at the height of his career and Ben Sherman himself passed away in 1987, such were their achievements that both names echo down the years more strongly than ever.

Another success story is that of Rio Ferdinand. Raised in South London, this major talent found success at West Ham and Leeds before joining the biggest club in Britain, if not the world, Manchester United. Clothes have always played a big part in Rio's life, representing as he does with great style, today's urban youth. With the Ben Sherman company expanding their clothing range, Rio is the perfect model for this development, a natural clothes horse and keen stylist who can marshal his wardrobe as beautifully as he does the United's defence.

Calum Best in a Ben Sherman T-shirt featuring father George

GEORGE BEST PROMO PLAYING CARD, THE ACE - NATURALLY!
GEORGE BEST BEN SHERMAN RANGE OF CLOTHING TAGS,
CALUM BEST WEARING HIS DAD, AS SEEN IN THE *DAILY MIRROR*

THE ORDINARY BOYS, 2004
FROM L-R: CHARLIE, WILL, PRESTON AND JAMES
PHOTOGRAPHY BY DAVID ELLIS

"My older brother turned me on to Ben Shermans - just like most other good things in life: guitars, The Clash, girls...I like Ben Shermans because they cross subcultures - desired as much by boy racers as they are by music fans or sports enthusiasts. Bens always look good, despite whatever trends and fads are around. Brighton and Hove museum had a display of Ben Sherman clothes through the last 40 years and I noticed that I owned a red checked short-sleeved Ben identical to one on a photo of a young suedehead from the late '70s. It was a charity shop affair so I like to think that I have THAT very shirt with THAT history. But I suppose the Ben Sherman label adds that history to every item of clothing they produce."

PRESTON
THE ORDINARY BOYS

1 2 3 4 can I have a

"Ben Sherman are proud to represent the
greatest band of all time - The Beatles.
The Fab Four and Ben Sherman... absolutely
the very best of British.

little more?
(LENNON & McCARTNEY)

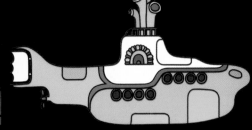

We suspect that Ben Sherman's association with
The Beatles must be the envy of every clothing
manufacturer in the world - and quite right too!"

JAMIE HALL - BEN SHERMAN

NORMAN COOKS UP A STORM

MY vote for top act went to NORMAN COOK (left).

Better known as FATBOY SLIM, he slipped quietly on to the bill under the name Drunk Soul Brother.

Norman's head-to-head with the CHEMICAL BROTHERS was brilliant. Meanwhile, FRANZ FERDINAND (below, right) and SCISSOR SISTERS (below) battled it out for the accolade Best Band.

On Friday Franz really got things going and had everyone jumping along to the likes of Take Me Out.

But the Scissors played two shows and the first, on Saturday, really lifted rain-dampened spirits.

Other great sets came from BASEMENT JAXX, ZERO 7, BLACK EYED PEAS (right) and KINGS OF LEON.

SPALDING ROCKWELL NEARLY WEARING
BEN SHERMAN WOMENSWEAR!
PHOTOGRAPHY BY DAVID YELLEN - C/O ARCREPS NY.
WARDROBE STYLING BY JAMIE ROSENTHAL

Ben Sherman now enjoys 'cult' status in the USA, and is one of the coolest brands to wear in New York City. This desirability is reflected in the distribution of Ben Sherman in New York - Bloomingdales, Fred Segals, Michael K in SoHo, and the type of product bought; smart Crombie's, boating blazers, ultra slim-fit shirts and trousers. The Ben Sherman office attracts a huge amount of interest from celebrities and bands such as The Rapture, The Vines, Blink 182 & Ashton Kutcher and due to expansion, will soon be moving to Union Square, to the same building that was once home to Andy Warhol's legendary Factory. The first USA Ben Sherman store will open in New York by the end of 2005 selling the complete Ben Sherman offering: Denim, Footwear, Womenswear, Accessories and of course, Shirts. Its an absolute joy to hang out with our New York colleagues and meet new Ben Sherman fans. Indeed the ghost of Ben Sherman takes the brand full circle - making his mark in the US, again.

SARAH FEENEY
BEN SHERMAN
UK MARKETING
MANAGER.

NEW YORK, 2004 - BEN SHERMAN USA AND GQ MAGAZINE PUT ON A PARTY
TO CELEBRATE AN INSTALLATION OF ORIGINAL PHOTOS BY RESPECTED
NY PHOTOGRAPHER DAVID YELLEN. BLOOMINGDALES HOUSED THE EVENT
AS PART OF THEIR STORE LAUNCH IN SOHO.

FROM TOP -
MICHAEL BUCKLEY (CEO - USA) AND PRINCESS SUPERSTAR,
DANA DYNAMITE (NEW YORK PR MANAGER) WITH SUPERMODEL AND GQ COVER GIRL KAROLINA KURKOVA,
DAVID YELLEN AND HALF OF NEW YORK CLUB PROMOTERS MOTHER FUCKER,
SPALDING ROCKWELL.

TOP RIGHT, THE INVITE FOR THE GQ PARTY AT BLOOMINGDALES - SOHO,
BOTTOM RIGHT, SARAH FEENEY AND COLIN BRICKLEY (LA PRODUCT PLACEMENT)
OUTSIDE BLOOMINGDALES ON RESTORED LAMBRETTA SX 200

THE RAVEONETTES
PHOTOGRAPHY BY DAVID YELLEN - C/O ARCREPS NY.
WARDROBE STYLING BY JAMIE ROSENTHAL

"Ben Sherman has always represented all things Mod to me, Carnaby Street, Swinging London. If you're at all interested in cultural movements... I mean music, art, design, style and fashion, then you can't avoid stumbling across Ben Sherman. It's cultural history."

SHARIN FOO:
THE RAVEONETTES

"Ben Sherman?
Mod, sexy and Klassy -
with a capital K!"

DJ PRINCESS SUPERSTAR
models Ben Sherman
womenswear

PRINCESS SUPERSTAR
PHOTOGRAPHY BY DAVID YELLEN - C/O ARCREPS NY.
WARDROBE STYLING BY JAMIE ROSENTHAL

Ben Sherman®

40TH BIRTHDAY PARTY

You are invited to our exclusive street party celebrating 40 years of Ben Sherman

Good Ol' Fashioned Knees Up! WEDNESDAY 17TH SEPTEMBER 2003

At Canvas, King's Cross Goods Yard, off York Way, London N1. Entertainment starts from 7.30pm

The Extravaganza Includes:

LIVE BANDS & DJS REPRESENTING ICONIC BRITISH MUSIC FROM THE PAST 40 YEARS

Traditional East End Landlord
Plus Other Acts
Real Ale, Fish & Chips
Mod Movie Moments & More

XIS WILL BE AVAILABLE FROM THE VENUE ON THE NIGHT
NVITATION ONLY. PLEASE BRING THIS INVITE TO GAIN ENTRY
SvP party@bensherman.co.uk Tel: 020 7812 5300

ADMIT ONE

TOM LOXLEY + VICTORIA
MAXIM

AHA + CREW
SUGARBABES STYLIST

SMART DOGS

Mark Lamarr

JIMMY HASSELBAINK

KOFI SO SOLID

CLANGER
LIBERTY X STYLIST

ASHLEY — VICE

TIM FROM DAZED
DAZED & CONFUSED

ROOTS — FAMILY
ROOTS MANUVA

Ollie Picton Jones
THE MIRROR

TIM + LINDA
VIVIENNE WESTWOOD

NEVILLE STAPLE
THE SPECIALS

THE SALON

MEL ROBERTS
MAXIM

JMB — FAMILY
UNIVERSAL RECORDS

MICHAEL CLEARY
& LOADED CREW

TOM BOTTOMLEY
DRAPERS

TOP: MILES GRAY AND LINFORD
ABOVE: SNAPSHOTS OF A GREAT 40th BIRTHDAY PARTY...

BEN SHERMAN 40TH BIRTHDAY PARTY

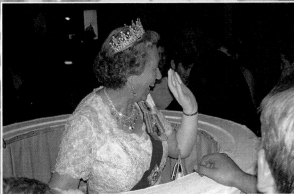

C/W FROM TOP: THE SPECIALS WOW THE CROWD AT THE 40th BIRTHDAY PARTY (THE LINE UP INCLUDED: NEVILLE STAPLE, RANKING ROGER (THE BEAT), CHAS SMASH (MADNESS), ANDY PERRISS, TIM VOAT, ROB COATES, JOE ATKINSON, WARREN MIDDLETON, COLIN GRAHAM, MIKE GINGOLD, TONY LANKIN, JANICE HOYTE, ANDRE SHAPPS, IAN WATA)
BEN SHERMAN GIRL ON A RESTORED LAMBRETTA LI OUTSIDE PARTY VENUE, COURTESY OF THE ODD MOD SQUAD SC
LIBERTY X ENTERTAIN THE GUESTS, 'THE QUEEN' ARRIVES! - ALL PARTY PHOTOS: JOHANNA PARKIN

DAY OFF
FUZZY AND CASUAL
LEAVING A
HOLLYWOOD THEATER

#733 • October 17, 2003

Entertainment
WEEKL

OSCAR
SHOWDOW
Can Big Studios
Crush Little Movie

Jack
Black
He's
The
Man!

With SCHOOL
OF ROCK The
Class Clown
Becomes
A Hollywood
Superstar

HACKM

HOFFM
They R
Each Othe
Mov

LUTH
VANDRO
Will the
Piper of L
Sing Aga

www.ew.com (AOL Keyword: EW)

$3.50 (CAN. $4.50)

43

0 74470 10210 0

OPPOSITE: VARIOUS PRESS CLIPPINGS FEATURING, C/W FROM TOP LEFT:
ANDRE 3000, ASHTON KUTCHER, A KING OF LEON, 2 LINKIN PARKS, JACK BLACK, THE RAPTURE, MIKE SKINNER (THE STREETS)
THIS PAGE FROM TOP: BLOOMINGDALES NYC WINDOW DISPLAY, CARNABY STREET STORE X 3, CARNABY STREET STORE, GEORGE BEST WINDOW AT CARNABY STREET, BERLIN STORE,
BEAMS STORE TOKYO, OXFORD STREET SYDNEY STORE X 2

As a Great British lifestyle brand Ben Sherman was proud to announce its partnership with the British Olympic Association. As the official formalwear supplier to Team GB athletes and officials, Ben Sherman provided a wide range of products and accessories that included suits, casual and formal shirts, ties, footwear, underwear, socks, belts, ladies' handbags, cufflinks and a commemorative dog tag, all designed specifically for the British Team, to encourage, motivate and inspire them for the Olympic Games Athens 2004.

"I first heard about
Ben Shermans when I was
at school in Manchester.
They were the coolest shirts to have,
and everyone wanted the button-downs.
Ben Sherman always seem to get the
balance right between trendy and smart.
My favourite Ben Sherman item is my
parka though - exactly the same
as my son's."

DARREN CAMPBELL:
ATHLETE

"Over the last seven years at Ben Sherman I have been overwhelmed when every time I mention the Ben Sherman name, people from all walks of life have fond memories of their first Ben Sherman shirt, where they bought it and how good they felt about owning one. In fact it was these short stories that inspired us to create this book. My Dad bought me my first Ben Sherman shirt in the mid-60s at a store in my local town, Aldershot. I remember distinctly it was a red and white check and I felt really cool wearing it. The store was Edgar Jerome and I am pleased to say that it is still in business and a faithful stockist of Ben Sherman. This little personal anecdote reflects the longevity and affection associated with the Ben Sherman brand. I am truly privileged to be running such a great British company."

MILES GRAY:
CHIEF EXECUTIVE, BEN SHERMAN

"Rap is about style. Through their poetry rappers talk specifically about what is cool. With Jay-Z it's those dress shirts he's wearing - Ben Sherman - with jeans. That's what we're doing in the hood right now."

RUSSELL SIMMONS:
FOUNDER OF DEF JAM AND PHAT FARM
FROM THE SPRING/SUMMER 2004 FHM COLLECTIONS U.S.

"Actually I came across Ben Sherman in England on one of my many trips there but the brand was re-introduced in the US by Dana Dynamite in 2000 and we have been tight ever since. I love the fact that they have nice clothes, not just T-shirts but dressy pieces for all occasions... I really enjoy the fresh colours, updated designs, and slick fabrics they use for their clothes. I also love the fact that Ben Sherman does not use their logo in a unfashionable manner."

DJ SNEAK: RECORD PRODUCER & DJ

A SMALL SELECTION OF BEN SHERMAN ADVERTISING PLANNED FOR 2005

"I had always associated Ben Sherman with men's shirts and I remember my boyfriends, when I was a teenager, desperate to wear them. I didn't realise they made equally stylish and comfortable clothes for the lady in good colours, all nicely tailored, femine but comfortable. My Ben Sherman stripey blazers are my fave though. I actually have three - one red & navy blue, one light blue & dark blue and one cream & pink. Great with jeans and a t-shirt or dressed up with a demin skirt and boots."

EDITH BOWMAN:
DJ & PRESENTER

"When did I discover Ben Sherman? Officially, this morning. Sometimes I'm a little slow on the uptake. I wondered where all these cool clothes ca
Now I know it's Ben Sherman! I like them because they're understated, and most of the clothes don't scream 'Look at me, I'm trendy!' yet the
panache." WAYNE KRAMER: MC5 / "I think the clothes and the company are based upon ideals that are sound; excess, mischief and living lif
the radar. When I wear Ben Sherman clothes I feel like I have class. There's also something to be said about being dressed smart and w
clothes that actually fits a man's body." TOMMIE SUNSHINE / "Post punk, youth-wear had yet to reach the suburbs in 1977. In Romford
available in fashion shops was mainstream, i.e. whatever David Essex, or ABBA were wearing! The Ben Shermans in these shops wou
collared variety, huge rounded collars normally in garish colours or loud prints! I remember me and Jeff Shadbolt trawling the Help the
and sometimes Brick Lane flea market for those elusive button-down pointed collar Ben Shermans with the essential pleat dow
any particular favourite, but of course that style was back in the mainstream a couple of years later!" SIMON STEBBING: PURP
forget your first football match, shag and Ben Sherman." ANON / "I was born in London, but after spending most of my life ic
my life in a funny way. It all came to me when my grandparents from London brought me a gift. A Ben Sherman Polo. Skatir
my Benny, I had no clue what history I was a part of - the feel and colours and tradition. It gave the kids something to
fashion. Ben Sherman has stayed true to its roots and it has lasted through time. A true classic in a plastic world." ROLA
shirt for New Years Eve....everywhere I went in this shirt I got comments. This is where it gets good. My friends and I
and hit a club for some dancing and as I'm getting drunk at the bar, these two girls come up and start talking to me
gives me her number to call her up later on, but when she's not looking, her friend slips me her cell number as w
them. The friend knows and doesn't care, the short one has no idea at all. Blame Ben Sherman!" ROBERT KINC
of the past with projections of the future. That there is a good historical understanding, very nostalgic but
that grew from the Mod movement, which was the working-class outsmarting the upper class with a ser
don't notice it, it's very subtle, but it mixes a very straight classic style with something more bohemian
the immediate connection with the music scene. Initially it was the jazz and soul music collecting M
with Britpop." SHARIN FOO - THE RAVEONETTES / "I sing for a Los Angeles based band called 'Trip'
the clothing line of the companies that endorse us. Ben Sherman clothes rock! Pure and sim
anywhere without getting attention (especially from the ladies). Our fresh new look (thanks to
for a long time - style! I actually hooked up with a *Playboy* centrefold after she approached
my clothes and fashion sense, and the next thing I knew we were off for sushi! I may nev
Sherman changed my life... thanks Ben! P.S. We'd love to talk about an endorsement, b
be endorsed by a clothing line we are not jazzed about!" RA TRIP NAVARRO / "I first re
Slade country! It was 1975/76 and we were all skinheads, listening to Trojan - blue
who had to do the dirty work. I remember how neat and cool the older kids wer
the local washing lines became common place. We would skive off school & l
tale plumes of steam of a mum doing some washing, then wait... Soon as th
over the hedge or fence to grab them and disappear with our booty. You i
in someone elses shirt! Ha! I loved my short sleeved Bens and somewhe
trousers. Keep your eyes peeled for them hedge hoppers!" PAUL RAVE
all the comprehensive school rude boys would come past the gates
one day they gave me a gingham short sleeve Ben Sherman. Was
about this style, that style, this season, that year... Forget abou
always made me feel good. I always felt so smart and nicely
WOODHEAD, BRIGHTON MOD, 1960s / "In 1976, when I was
liked the little details - the pleat down the back and t
respect." MICHAEL WATSON: BOXER / "My family has
on my birthday. I almost drowned in one of his pool
Beatles' *Yellow Submarine* on them and other un
is Mod fashion but being from San Diego, we d
scooters, and I guess there are some cool 60
who got in fights with the punks, but it wa
in David Bowie and things like that. Part
married to an awsome French woman
THE RAPTURE / "My friend and I ope
Shermans though, no matter what
We actually look forward to iro
a Ben Sherman shirt...thank
Shermans. She was a fash
remember the month and
moment, in that Nordst
or dinner. But it's cas
in that shirt. I wore
good - which, I'
shirt feels the
My favourit
wear this
was ab
Sher
cla
c

shirts. They were his trademark and she wasn't. She had to go." JON SCOTT BLANTHORN: WRITER - EXCERPT FROM ARTICLE, ELLE CANADA, JUNE 2004 / "The placket was a criss cross sort of diamond shape pattern down the front. Which you don't see on the modern ones… it was made separately. It was got rid of because it was easier to make the shirts without putting an extra piece on the front." JOHN BYRNE: BRIGHTON SKINHEAD 1970 - PRESENT DAY / "Among the striped ones I owned, there was a wide blue/white long sleeve that I never saw anyone else wearing. The material even had a special smell when you ironed it. I was so proud wearing it at the Tottenham Royal with my sleeveless v-neck, sta-prest and highly polished brogues. Small details were really important like the sleeves rolled up twice. Every Saturday we would browse for records and clothes, but we would always end up at Davis's in Tottenham High Road, which had a huge Ben Sherman selection even if it was enemy territory for us Arsenal fans! A few months after I had my first Ben Sherman it was hard to find something that set you apart from the hundreds of new skinheads appearing on the scene, so the quest was on to find a plain white Bennie. This I managed to do, and it was a good feeling to wear it, until the following week, when all my mates turned up in one! 30-odd years on I'm still wearing the Ben Shermans, but definitely not slim fit!" JIM COX, LONDON SKINHEAD FROM 1968 / "And I remember when samples started coming through with the square pleat at the back and the loop, and we all thought, 'What the hell is this?' He'd try anything new just to see if it would work!" JEAN IMRAY: BEN SHERMAN MACHINIST / "In my first year of college I had the opportunity to travel to London for the first time. My first stop was Carnaby Street. I had to buy some boots and braces and Ben Sherman button downs. My friends all left me behind. They were off seeking out tourist traps and waxworks. There was plenty of time for that. I filled my shopping bags with all the Ben Sherman shirts and sweaters I could afford and was amazed to be among people who understood it all." JAMES VINCENT: MAKEUP ARTIST / "At that time shirts were sold in dozens in boxes and he brought this idea from America of packaging them singly in a presentation box, mens shirts and it worked, they sold well, Ben Sherman shirts, that was how it all started…he showed me one and I said 'Oh don't be daft, shirts come in dozens' you know…but it was a winner, he knew." JACK LYONS: BEN SHERMAN'S UNCLE / "Ben Sherman shirts are the coolest in the world. At 13 I wanted a black and white checked one for Christmas. My mother got me a black and white checked shirt, but it wasn't a Ben Sherman! I was jealous as fuck when my mate Colin came round sporting his new one. Since then I've never let my mother buy clothes for me. It was great when Ben Sherman returned, it was like meeting an old school pal you haven't seen in ages. They are proper, old school boy-wear and I've never got one off my back. I'll even keep it on when I make love. Ben Sherman rules ya bass!" IRVINE WELSH: AUTHOR / "It may be of interest to you that I knew Ben Sherman quite well. At the time I was working in a travel agents in Brighton and he had a workshop above Burtons in West Street and he used to sometimes bring in Irish workers and I used to handle all his travel. In fact when he first produced his check button-down shirts he brought a pink and a green one into me and asked what I thought of them and then gave them to me for my then boyfriend! I was very popular in Brighton!" GERALDINE: BRIGHTON MOD / "It was the day after The Jam, under the name of John's Boys, played a secret gig at The Marquee - I was among the many 'tickets' without a ticket and couldn't get in. The day after, as consolation, I had my hard earned Saturday job money in my pocket and I went up East Ham High Street and after much humming and hawing about the expense, I bought a Ben Sherman button-down I'd seen in the window of an old blokes' outfitters - bright petrol blue, in a really soft Oxford cloth. Beautiful. I think it must have been there for years as it had a bigger, more rolled collar than most of the ones I'd seen around. Walking home, feeling light in my hush-puppies with my purchase, I was accosted by a gang of older skins outside Woolworths. They were going to either mug me or thump me, so I stood against Woolies wall with the bag behind my back ready for a kicking... I got grabbed from both sides and they were deciding who was going to hit me first when one of them asked what was in the bag - after a pause for courage I said it was a Ben Sherman, and if they wanted it they would have to fucking well try and take it. 'A fucking Ben Sherman mate?' he says, 'Let's have a look.' Reluctantly I got the shirt out to nods of appreciation from these guys. 'You're alright mate - we'll catch you another day.' he said with a laugh as they all bowled off, giving me a friendly twat round the head as he and his mates passed. Why they didn't just take the shirt off me I don't know. Maybe a respect for the label. Whatever the reasons they didn't and I never did see them again, but to this day I still thank Christ, my Guardian Angel - and Ben Sherman - for making me spend that money on that shirt. Lifesaver." PAUL McEVOY: GRAPHIC DESIGNER / "My favourite Ben Sherman was, and still is, a lovely sky blue button-down which got loads of use on stage... and at weddings, funerals etc. I still have it but alas it no longer fits. But I keep it in pride of place in the wardrobe, you see I'm always the optimist." GARY SPARKS: PURPLE HEARTS / "It would have a placket front which most shirts didn't have at that time, it would have a button down collar which most shirts didn't have at that time and the collar had quite a roll on it, you know … And of course they did all those pale colours which were quite flattering. The pinks and the blues and lilacs and greens and things… I mean, a pale pink shirt was considered really outrageous." MICHAEL LOWRIE: BUYER FOR THE GOG SHOP, BRIGHTON, MID-LATE 1960s / "A lot of the time if you're going to a special music night you get suited and booted: shirt, suit, shoes, socks, all the attention to detail... it's the shirt that finishes the whole idea." DAVE 'DIZZY' COOKE / "I first came across Ben Shermans - Oh! That sounds naughty! I've never met this Ben Sherman person! No really, let's say I 'discovered' Ben Shermans at the Rose Bowl flea market in LA. They have an English sensibility that at the same time seems very Southern California. That's really cool. You do the math." CARSON KRESSLEY: QUEER EYE FOR THE STRAIGHT GUY / "I bought my first Ben Sherman in a shop in Old Compton Street in Soho. It was a button down with a turquoise and blue check design. Classic. I like to buy clothes that don't date, so you could say I'm a follower of style and quality - not just fashion. I still wear the shirts these days. Even my son likes them!" CARL WAYNE: THE MOVE / THE HOLLIES / "I first started wearing Ben Shermans in 1968. I liked the button down collars and the short sleeves. Ben Shermans have an instantly recognisable style, with the trademark pleat on the back. My favourite shirt right now is an all black BS. I wear it all the time. Plus I also still have the white BS I got married in 14 years ago! How's that for customer loyalty?" ROB HINGLEY (AKA BUCKET): THE TOASTERS / "You used to iron it and you could smell… even though it had been washed it still had a Ben Sherman smell." BOB SPENCER: BRIGHTON SKINHEAD 1970 / "As an original mod from the 60's now living in San Francisco, I keep looking for those original Ben Sherman shirts that were striped in really super colours, like peppermint green with red and white thin stripes... I remember buying my Shermans from the David Argent boutique in Crawley, Sussex... super mod shop in the 60's. Unfortunately long gone now!" BARRY JONES / "I first came across Ben Shermans when I was 16 in Manchester. I loved the way even the roughest, hard nut kids from Salford looked polished on a night out with a button down, dark Levi's and Reeboks. My favourite has got to be my classic blue and white check button down Oxford. The Ben Sherman brand has an interesting heritage and has been a big influence on the way many subcultures dress for decades." ANDREW DAVIES: *ARENA* FASHION EDITOR / "My earliest memory of Ben Sherman Shirts was in 1971 at the young age of 12 years old. I had just started Secondary School and after a few months into the school term I was assigned a project on Industry within Northern Ireland. The class was divided into teams of four boys. Our team were handed 'The Shirt Industry within Derry'. Our project focused in on the Ben Sherman factory at Maureen Avenue, which wasn't that far from our school. I prepared some notes about the factory and arranged an interview with the factory manager, whose name I have since forgotten. A few days later the school team of four scruffy kids assembled sheepishly into the manager's office and we kicked off the 'interview'. About half an hour into these high profile discussions the factory manager offered us some tea and biscuits; we couldn't believe our luck, this was excellent, we had made it; forget about the project we got tea and biscuits. I bet no other team got offered tea and biscuits. News even reached our school before we left the Ben Sherman factory. The next day back at school I was summoned to the principal's office, something about our visit to the Ben Sherman factory. I thought, 'shit, someone must have nicked all the biscuits, broken a cup, spilt the milk or worse'. Well I needn't have worried, in fact I was congratulated by the principal. Apparently the factory manager phoned our school the next day to say that he was very impressed with our visit. I think he may have even offered me a position within the company when I finished school. Happy days indeed. It wasn't until seven years later, when The Undertones were blasting their way through the hit parade that I bought my first Ben Sherman shirt. This was something that you aspired to. I could never afford such high fashion gear until then. I loved the shirts, even wearing them on *Top Of The Pops*. I even wore a Ben Sherman shirt on my wedding, a body hugging white button-down collar shirt, very nice. During the early 1980s The Undertones rehearsed in Chambers Refrigeration, a local air conditioning company whose premises butted right up to the Ben Sherman factory in Maureen Avenue; the very same factory where I got tea and biscuits as a young schoolboy. Throughout the career of The Undertones I have always and still wear Ben Sherman shirts. The Undertones even had friends and family working in the Ben Sherman factories in Derry. If Ben Sherman keep making them, then I'm still wearing them." BILLY DOHERTY: THE UNDERTONES

Ben Sherman would like to thank everyone for their contributions to this book.

Special thanks to all the team at Rude Boy Music and to Neville Staple who releases his new album "The Rude Boy Returns" together with a DVD in September. Check out www.rudeboymusic.co.uk for all the current information on Neville and the label, plus up-to-date tour information.

Thanks:
Miles, Andy, Sarah, Zoë, Charlotte, Martin, Jamie, Dana and all the gang at Ben Sherman, Daphne Sherman for her interviews and reference material, Angela Charles for her sterling research, all the button-down heroes (they know who they are) who went to the trouble to supply us with quotes, memories and invaluable button-down information, Paul, Julien & Julie Mc at Bold - business as usual! NFA Archive and Phil Smee at Strange Things Picture Library for some great archive shots, Andy Gillard at Scootering, Lambretta Lee, Paul Hallam, Bob Morris, Steve Woof @ EMI, Alan Parker, Andy 'Spellcheck' Neill, Keith Badman, Eddie Piller, Jim Guynan and Ian Jones for trying, Gary Crowley, Steve Diggle and the guys for sweating blood - literally, The Get Go - who played a blinder, Sarah Bacon, Rob Harvey at Lola for football and fine wines, Chris Charlesworth, Guy Lloyd, Susan Currie, Paul Klinker, Buddy Ascott, Billy Hassett & Martin Mason, Gary Sparks, Jeff Shadbolt & Simon Stebbing, Dave Cairns for his insights, Hayden at MPH for resurrecting the Macintosh... cheers.

Sincere apologies to anyone we might have inadvertently forgotten.

All trade marks used in this book are respectfully acknowledged.